LOVE IN METRO

LOVE IN METRO

Arun Anand

Ocean Paperbacks
A Division of Ocean Books Pvt. Ltd.
ISO 9001:2008 Publishers

Published by
Ocean Paperbacks
A Division of Ocean Books Pvt. Ltd.
4/19 Asaf Ali Road,
New Delhi-110 002 (INDIA)
e-mail: info@oceanbooks.in

ISBN 978-81-8430-181-6
Love in Metro
by Arun Anand

Edition
First, 2013

Price
Rs. 125.00 (Rupees One Hundred Twenty Five only)

Printed at
Bhanu Printers, Delhi

For all those
who are yet to
find their soulmates

Contents

1

Time will tell: End or Beginning?

Was it the end or was it the beginning? He didn't know. Neither would you nor me. Time will tell.

He reached at the Metro Station and started waiting for her. Despite the cool air conditioning and not so hot weather of September he was sweating profusely.

What a bizarre idea this is for a grown up man to run away with a girl and that too…… after so much has happened, thought Pankaj.

"As a journalist, I have reported so many stories where girls and boys ran away and never came back. But this is sounding even more bizarre to me. I just cannot imagine that I am going to Mussoorie with a young woman who I know only for 13 months," Pankaj was thinking.

Thoughts were travelling faster than the metro trains which were zipping past the platform where he was standing.

He just checked his watch again. He will have to wait for another half-an-hour. He had reached here quite early, much earlier than anyone could have expected.

He could not sleep last night. He was a little fatigued but still felt like a live electric wire. It is a heady cocktail—the feeling of doing something bizarre and turning your life upside down coupled with mental fatigue which generally is the result of long winding thoughts clashing with each other when one takes such a bold and bizarre decision.

You feel you are on a high while also realising that if you fall, there would be no chance of recovery. It is one giant leap into future full of uncertainties.

Memories were coming back to his mind like waves hit the shores with chaotic energy. Memories of his parents bringing him up with such a great effort and even greater love.

Memories of the way his investigative stories were appreciated by his colleagues, friends and families, memories sipping hot-sweet tea with Sameera on wintry nights at "Jai Hind" tea stall near their office.

Memories of his drinking bouts with Varun, beer binges with colleagues, getting up bleary eyed with terrible hangovers for chasing the stories.

No one, not even he himself, could have ever imagined that he would be leaving his home, his friends, his city, his profession, for a girl.

He had to cut off everything and go to a different world right now. He knew his parents would be surprised to get a call from him from Mussoorie.

For the time being, what is important for him is Nisha. They had decided that they would meet at 5 p.m. at Rajiv Chowk Metro Station. From there they would change the Metro and go to Kashmere Gate. Here they would get down and take a private inter-state bus to Mussoorie. They had got their seats reserved. The bus would leave at around 8 p.m. and they would reach Mussoorie in morning at around 6 a.m.

And then a new life would begin. But how good this would be? What will happen to his parents? His mother would be shattered, his father may not be able to take it.

His confidence was a little shaken now and he was having second thoughts about what he was going to do. He wanted to cry and laugh at the same time while feeling a numbness that was wearing him out emotionally.

Then he saw her walking towards him. Wasn't she wearing the same blue jeans and white shirt which made her look like an angel 13 months ago. If he could see himself in the mirror, he had a strange lopsided smile on his face. He couldn't just believe for a moment that he was living such a bizarre story.

❑

2

Coup de foudre!

He had become conscious of the fact that someone's knee was touching his knee. It was not unusual in Delhi's Metro trains to grapple with arms, knees, feet of fellow travellers. But what made Pankaj conscious was the fact that there was this beautiful young woman sitting by his side and it was her knee.

It was 11.30 a.m. in the morning and yet there was so much rush. It is suprising, he thought.

The rush hour lasted from 8.30 to 10.30 a.m. He was lucky to be working in a newspaper where you can afford to reach office in afternoon and leave late in the evening, especially if you are working in editorial department and that too reporting.

Pankaj had spent three years in this profession as a correspondent in a leading English newspaper in the city. It was one of the leading newspapers in the city and he was reporting on civic amenities. In journalistic parleys, it could be said that Pankaj was covering "civic amenities" as a beat. (Every functional area assigned for coverage to the regular reporters is called a beat. And just like beat constables, thus, you find beat reporters too. Funny? The main beats in a city reporting department in a newspaper or news channel comprise mainly of crime, education, health, politics, government, civic bodies/

---

* 'Love at first sight' (Coup de foudre' is a french expression for "Love at first sight)

civic amenities, entertainment and lifestyle).

He was young, average looking with a little unruly hair. He was in the habit of keeping his hair short though his mother never liked that. Pankaj smiled every time she told him, "You are very good looking my son, you will look even better if you will allow your head to have a little more hair." But Pankaj somehow felt unhygienic as soon his hair grew a little bit. He was a little different from other fellows of his age in this regard at least.

The train of his thoughts got disrupted as the metro suddenly screeched to a halt and the young woman's knee pressed even harder. Now Pankaj was really uncomfortable. He didn't know what to do. The woman was sitting pretty as if nothing had happened. Probably she was used to it and didn't bother much.

This 'cold blooded' behaviour of his fellow passenger reminded him of how his female colleagues who worked with him often complained of unruly behaviour of passengers and the way used to ensure that all the women travellers, especially the younger ones didn't get down from the metro without cursing themselves for being born this city without enough wealth to have chauffeur driven car that could take them to office everyday.

Pankaj stole a glance at the young woman even as the heavily accented pre-recorded voice was informing passengers in Hindi, "*yatra seva mein thoda vilamb hoga*". It was immediately followed by another heavily accented pre-recorded female voice in English which informed, "There will be a short-delay" in this train journey.

Pankaj decided to steal a glance at the young woman. He looked at her from the corner of his eye. She was a ravishing beauty. Clad in blue jeans and white top with little make-up visible on her face, she had long straight hair that fell on her shoulders, a sharp nose with big bright eyes. She had grace, class and innocence. Her age was any body's guess—could be anything between 22 years to 26 years.

What could he do? He was stunned. He took a deep breath without realizing that he had done so. Something was happening. He didn't know what? Something was there. Is it "*Coup de foudre*?" It means "love at first sight" in French.

"Now why the hell you have to think of all these expressions about love in French, *angrezi me bolo na yaar,* Sameera, his best friend in the office used to scold him. But that was the only way Pankaj could ensure that he would remember and revise a few expressions from the weekend classes he took for learning French at Alliance Francaise in Delhi.

So my dear is it "*Coup de foudre*", Pankaj was asking himself. From Rajouri Garden to Rajiv Chowk it took him 25 minutes for the journey.

Two years and more than, 700 trips to and fro from a Metro Station, as he often used to count, from Rajouri Garden Metro Station to Rajiv Chowk Station had made him witness to myriad colours of life often painted with more grey shades than the brighter ones. He realised people were stressed, tense, ready to fight with anyone for no reason. They behaved more like aggressive machines. Old or young, men or women, it didn't matter. They were all running, chasing something. Their laughter was superficial. The young ones giggled, the older ones could sometime force a smile or two but they all looked worried, very worried and insecure. That is why while travelling in metro, Pankaj enjoyed when kids come along with their parents. They would jump on the seats, often irritate some passengers too, but at the end of it they were the ones who brought cheer to many faces.

He had observed as soon as kids entered a metro coach, the atmosphere appeared to be lighter and brighter. He had told the Public Relation Officer (PRO) of Delhi Metro recently on phone while talking to him about some story, "Get more kids in Delhi Metro buddy and you would reduce stress of thousands of Delhities atleast for a few minutes."

From Rajiv Chowk, it took him, ten minutes walk to reach his office. He must have seen several hundred girls during these trips. He liked some, was almost ready to fall in love with a few but this had never happened. The warmth of her body was engulfing him, pervading him, piercing him, just taking him away from himself.

He didn't realise that during the last five minutes the train had not moved an inch. People were getting restless. They had started cursing Metro. "*Aji kya faayda iska, blue line waala haal hai* (what is the use of having a metro, its just like blueline – a public transport system comprising of privately run buses which ravaged city roads for more than one and a half decade till 2010)," said a grumpy balding chap who must be in his forties. He must be a trader in Karol Bagh. They are the ones who can be recognized by their heavily accented Punjabi.

From cricket to inflation, they would comment on each and everything, hardly allowed others to speak, talked on their cell phones quite loudly about "money matters" making sure people all around should be aware that they have made money.

Pankaj was a Punjabi too but probably the academic atmosphere at his home had ensured that he didn't become as brash as Karol Bagh wallahs though West Delhi was the hub of "Panju culture" which all his non-Punjabi colleagues scorned at in office. Pankaj took these barbs sportingly with a smile as he knew there was lot of truth in the fact that "Panjus", as many upper middle class Punjabis were known in Delhi, were quite brash and never left an opportunity to show off their wealth.

A common joke he had heard about this culture at his home was, "If you are a true Panju, you would not loose an opportunity to tell how much real estate wealth you have even if you are having a conversation with a complete stranger not lasting more than five minutes!"

Meanwhile, the train started moving. The air conditioning was better. And then something happened which appeared to be trivial and of no consequence initially but which would have a profound impact on Pankaj's life.

How could this young man know that a trivial thing like cough can shake your world, change your world, transform it completely.

But this cough appeared. And probably God wanted this young woman to have it. She was not eating, neither chewing gum nor munching a chocolate, she was not talking furiously, like many others in the same coach, on her cell phone and yet something got stuck in her throat. She coughed. And she coughed, coughed and coughed. First it was mild, then it became a little more pronounced, then it was like almost uncontrollable bringing tears to her eyes and allowing many passengers to start staring at her. How could they lose an opportunity to stare at a young woman in Delhi Metro.

As a thorough gentleman, which Pankaj always felt he was despite being a punju and troubling people often with the news stories he wrote against them, he took out a thermo-flask from his bag and offered water to her, a little meekly not knowing how she would react.

"Would you like to have some water?"

She was coughing badly by now.

There were tears in her eyes. She could only nod her head a little as she tried to curb her cough by covering her mouth with handkerchief.

He immediately put some water in the cap of the flask and offered her. She gulped it down. The cough improved. But still she was coughing. He poured some more water in the cap of the flask, she sipped it a little more patiently. And then the cough stopped. Meanwhile the announcement system informed. "This is Karol Bagh Metro Station. The doors will open on the left. Please mind the gap."

She gave back the cap. As Pankaj was putting the cap back on the flask, she thanked him, "God bless you, thanks." Pankaj noded his head and realised that the knee was not pressing anymore as she was sitting more comfortably now with large number of passengers getting down at Karol Bagh Metro Station.

They always do. Most of them are shoppers, shopkeepers, college students and workers on the shops in Karol Bagh Market which is one of the biggest markets in Delhi and an attraction for all those who visit Delhi. "You could do without going to Red Fort or Qutub Minar in Delhi, but if you are visiting Delhi and haven't shopped at Karol Bagh, you have wasted your trip to Delhi," one of his aunts in Chandigarh had told him few days ago as he drove them to Karol Bagh for a shopping extravaganza along with his cousins.

From Rajouri Garden, where Pankaj was born and brought up and continued to live with his parents, to Karol Bagh, journey on metro, provided there were no "short delays" took around 20 minutes. If one would have to travel by car it would take 50 minutes, the two-wheelers could chart the same course from 25 to 45 minutes.

The young ravishing beauty was wiping her face clean from the sweat beads that had appeared on her forehead. The metro moved on. Now there were only two stations left before Pankaj had to get down. First it would be "Jhandewalan" and then "Ramkrishna Ashram" after which the metro took underground route and reached Rajiv Chowk Station. Here people who wanted to go to Delhi University or old Delhi would get down and change the train. Those who wanted to go to the Central Secretariat, the showcase of notorious Indian babudom, would also get down.

Central Secretariat was a couple of kilometres away from the Parliament building. Just adjoining this was Press Club of India, a so-called exclusive club for journalists where one could get cheap liquor, lot of nonsense gossip and smell the stink that pervaded through corridors of the media world and spilled all over there. The glamour of media hides its deep, dirty underbelly. This Pankaj had realised during last three years.

Pankaj was bold enough now to steal glances more than often. He looked at his watch in between these glances. Five to six more minutes before his destination comes. Will it be one of those incidents which would once again take away his sleep for a couple of nights. It happened to him once in a while after seeing a beautiful young woman in metro.

He didn't know what to do with this streak inside him which made him fantasize about such women. He hadn't discussed it with anyone. Sometimes he got worried whether he was turning into a psycho, one of those who get desperate to have women. He had covered a few such cases and wrote some reports about them during the last three years.

"Damn it, it's going to be sleepless for the next couple of nights," he was thinking. Three minutes had passed since he last had a look at his watch. "Should I ask her name?," Pankaj thought. "What If I get snubbed, there are lot of people around. She may create a scene here. She might not respond even." His mind was ticking fast pondering various permutations and combinations. "She is so beautiful and smart. She will definitely have a boyfriend." His mind just didn't stop. His heart was beating a little faster. He could feel the sweat on the back of his neck despite decent air conditioning.

He was feeling a little feverish by now. He didn't know what to do. This happened to him initially when he was sent to cover big events by his newspaper as a cub reporter. That is what they call rookies in newspapers when they join as trainee reporters and they are made to cover each and every thing in the name of giving them a feel of all type of reporting assignments. Infact, these trainees are often used, manipulated and exploited by seniors to do the hardwork in the field and at the end of the day, they end up giving "inputs" for stories which are published under the names of senior journalists. The trainees' names does not figure anywhere. Their contribution goes unnoticed even as editors praise the senior reporters for all the hardwork they have put in to make a simple story look so special and better than news reports on the same event or incident or issue appearing in the rival newspapers.

After a few months, the trainees understand the real meaning of this popular saying in journalism, "You learn it the hard way in journalism." It actually means you continue to get exploited unless you become smart enough to start exploiting or atleast manipulating your junior colleagues and get away by passing the buck of such thankless assignments to others.

The young woman got up. She had smiled and said once again thanks to Pankaj.

"Did she or did she not?" Pankaj thought. His mind was now busy working out a pick-up line. Leave apart everything he was desperate to atleast know her name.

"Hi I am Pankaj, I am a journalist and work for…." "He had decided that he is going to say this first line to this woman right now.."

Jolt. Before he could blurt out this "golden line" which he had prepared with all his journalistic abilities, the metro halted with a slight jerk. The sliding doors opened in split second. The young woman had disappeared in the milieu. He could see a shade of white-T shirt.

Suddenly he realised he also has to get down. And he jumped from his seat but not without looking at something lying there. It was a mobile phone! He checked his mobile phone. It was there in his pocket. Then something struck him as lighting. *Coup de foudre*!!!!. It must be her cell phone. He grabbed it and got out of the metro coach just in time before the doors got shut. He had another look at the cell phone. It was the latest model of Nokia. He suddenly smiled as a billboard at the station just in front of him stared at him displaying in bold letters-**Nokia, Connecting People!**

❑

3

Calypso Calling

"If you are a physiotherapist, why do you need to collect cash, write receipts and convince prospective clients to join here," the question popped up once again in his mind as he looked at her while moving towards the lift. Only a half opened sliding glass door stopped him from reaching her. On the top right-hand side of the glass door, two words glittered- YOUR GYM.

What a funny name! Pankaj and Sameera had chuckled about this end number of times. Before visiting this gym he had always thought that anyone who holds a diploma or a degree in any stream of medical sciences can make lot of money. A single visit to this gym shattered his perception at least about physiotherapy being treated as an attractive profession for all and sundry.

This was one of the best gyms in the city. It had the best equipments, largest number of treadmills, sauna bath and steam facilities, well-trained smart trainers, a small lounge and a mysterious physiotherapist, to say the least, who haunted a young journalist's thoughts whenever he entered this building and had the chance to have a glance at her!

Potbelly businessman, tired middle-aged executives with layers of flesh bulging from their waists betraying their love for junk food and lot of booze and rich brats with smirk on their faces flocked it. It was a unisex gym like many such body building shops, which have sprung all over the city over the last few years. Zero sized aspiring models were found in ample numbers there. More than them were those women who aspired to be zero sized.

As moths are attracted to the fire, the trainers in the gyms were attracted to these women. The sophisticated ones chatted with them in English trying to give them more than professional advice. Often they showed their keenness to take some advice from them possibly outside the gym! Those who could not speak English fluently sulked and suffered and spent their time with other clients. These were largely boys from Haryana, Western Uttar Pradesh and from the border areas of Delhi. They came from villages or small towns. Delhi still has many villages largely located in what is known as "Outer Delhi". Did the name given to the geographical location of these villages itself is an indicator how they are considered to be 'out of place' by *Dilliwallahs*?

They looked gloomy, very gloomy. It was the same old story of growing divide between "haves" and the "have nots". So a few instructors in gym had many girls and women flocking to them and many of them had very few or no woman client to look after.

"You always find smart chics at the reception in such kind of places," Varun, Pankaj's pal in his colony, had told him once.

"This helps to increase the clientele, especially when it comes to enrolling rich, balding and utterly disfigured shop-owners and traders. You don't know their frustration level! I know some of them, so I do know their frustrations also. If a good looking woman is ready to have even a conversation with them, that give them enough kick everywhere.

Their wives have become obese and look more ugly than them. They don't work in BPOs and the KPOs, where they could meet some beautiful women. They run sultry godowns and wholesale shops or deal in real estate as property dealers. So what do you expect from them? They realise they have spent a life time earning money for the family, for themselves. Life has just bypassed them. They need someone to appreciate and recognise their existence not merely for their money but for what they are in bones and flesh, mind and spirit.

For their families they are no more than ATM machines. It is not the lust for women which is driving them crazy. More than that they want their youth back. And the more they try, the more desperate they become. But this is an illusion which keeps them alive and give them a notion of happiness. They are always hopeful, "*Koi to milegai jo hamare mote shareer ko nahin, hamare naram dil ko samjhegi*. (We will find someone who would not look at our out of shape body but at our velvet heart)."

Varun gave him this "*gyan*" over one of their drinking sessions few weeks ago. There was no dearth of "*gyan*" as far as Varun was concerned. He was worldly-wise. And even wiser when he was four drinks down with fifth in hand. As and when it happened, and it happened very often, he was always ready to finish the bottle. His '*gyan*' was directly proportional to the amount of booze which he consumed.

But this happens with most of us. Isn't it? Varun used to tell Pankaj (and this was his favourite "one-liner" there can be only two reactions after you consume good amount of liquor- either you will talk too much or you won't talk at all.) "*Yaar*, this the fun of drinking that you tend to go to extremes," Varun would say by the time he would be finishing the last one left in the bottle.

He was member of every club worth its name in the city, top health clubs and almost every five star gym worth its name in the town. What always surprised Pankaj during his early school days was that how Varun's father, who was a junior engineer in the Municipal Corporation of Delhi, had so much money to flaunt and splurge. Varun was making the best (or worst "it's a matter of perception" as Varun puts it always) use of his father's money since school days.

Pankaj had asked his father once, "Papa, you work in University as a professor I know your salary is much more than Varun's father then how come they have such big cars and such a big house and we have only one small car and a two bedroom house only."

Professor Manohar Lal Malhotra aka Professor M.L. Malhotra, had only patted on his back and smiled. What else he could do, as his twelve-year-old son was too small to understand how powerful a Junior Engineer is in a local civic body and how that power translates into moolah!

Pankaj came to know the answer once he started covering civic bodies in his newspaper. He knew by now that Varun's father was no different from hundreds of others of his tribe. No building plan gets a sanction, no house in this city gets constructed without greasing the palm of the local junior engineer in the civic body. This was one "industry" which always raked money, recession or no recession, it just didn't matter. It is always booming.

Pankaj shook his head and looked at the charming young woman sitting behind the reception counter at "YOUR GYM". He had talked to her once. His newspaper had sealed a corporate deal with this gym, which allowed employees in his organisation to get a 50 per cent discount on membership here.

They had laughed it out when the HR (Human Resources) Chief Amita Kala had sent a 450 words mail applauding the efforts made by her department (actually she meant herself!) in sealing this deal for the welfare of the employees.

So far, except for the complimentary membership to the Editor (Editors always get everything complementary!!) of his newspaper, around 20 more employees had taken this gym's membership.

Raghu Raj, the most lecherous of the Chief-sub Editors had told him over a drink at the bar in the Press Club, " I have taken YOUR GYM's membership to have a good look at the chics. Why else should I spend so much money? You get to see good chics there."

For Pankaj it was repulsive, for the rest of those who were surrounding Raghu Raj at the bar counter, it was a matter of great interest that his newspaper had a tie-up with a gym where good chics come. They were pleading with Raghu for some guest passes. Journalists are so used to getting everything for free here in India so why would they spare even a gym!

Two days after this session at the bar, Pankaj had gone to YOUR GYM with Sameera. She wanted to take membership and there she met Dr. Tanya. That is what she told her name was.

The encounter was vivid in his memory. Though it was hilarious but there was something, which was also ridiculous. In fact, in this city the line between hilarious and ridiculous is getting blurred. This often left Pankaj confused. This often leaves many of us confused even though we may not be able to understand this.

As Sameera and Pankaj had entered the gym, they met this young lady at the reception. With hair tied in a tight bun, a broad forehead, a small chain of pearls tugging her long neck, she had that typical PR (Public Relations) smile.

These smiles always made Pankaj uncomfortable as he thought how much these girls have to go through to earn the living.

"To smile and smile and be a pleasing personality always. It's difficult. You need to be yourself. You get paid for hiding your real feelings behind the garb of glittering smiles. Wow! This is the price, which millions pay in this world to hold on to jobs in organizations, which they hate from the core of their heart. Perhaps that is why they hate their organizations, their bosses even their colleagues at times as they just do not allow you to be sad, angry or even nonchalant," Pankaj wrote in his personal diary the day he went with Sameera to the gym.

Sameera was excited. "Hey Pankaj, I am going to give Kareena (Kapoor) a run for her money. Very soon I will be zero sized too," she told him while filling the forms.

As she placed her identity card in front of Dr. Tanya and said in a tone which had more authority than required, “Our newspaper has a deal with your gym for 50 per cent discount.”

Dr. Tanya raised her head slowly. The smile vanished. It came back again in flash and she almost fumbled, “Oh sure! Why not? Just wait for a second.” She went to a cabin whose door opened in the reception area itself. “Manager” the sign displayed in the middle of the cabin. She came back in three minutes, handed over Sameera her membership card as well as credit card with two slips, which had come out of the credit card machine. The amount charged was Rs 15,300. “Quite steep, even after the discount, Pankaj said.” Sameera nonchalantly said, “I can afford it yaar.”

As Sameera signed one of the credit card receipts and gave it back to the young lady at the reception She asked her, “What’s your name.” “Tanya, I mean Dr. Tanya.”

As soon as she said “Dr. Tanya”, the quintessential reporters-Pankaj and Sameera couldn’t stop a frown. They were rattled.

“I am a physiotherapist,” she said politely but confidently as she extended her hand. Both Pankaj and Sameera looked at each other. Sameera shook hands with her while Pankaj was shaking his head as both of them left saying without anything. As soon as they came out of the gym, the question popped between the two that if she is a physiotherapist why the hell is she acting as a receptionist. “Hey, I don’t mean to demean receptionists, but this baffles me. A physiotherapist doing client servicing for a gym?,” Pankaj asked Sameera.

“Struggle, Dude, Struggle, this is what you call struggle in life. A degree in physiotherapy doesn’t mean that you will land up with the best paying job in Max, Apollo or any such big hospital chain. You have to struggle hard. It’s no different for them.”

Pankaj frowned at these gems of knowledge being offered to him by Sameera. But he couldn’t keep the frown for long as he liked the way she spoke with an air of carelessness surrounding her.

One generally tends to search for such people who remain unguarded in conversations with you and one could remain unguarded with them while talking. They are the most valuable people in any office and generally most of the organizations do not have many such persons. Such unguarded conversations help to let off the steam. In fact, more than often, they are the most valuable people in our life too.

Isn't this the reason that we often share with strangers in a train or a bus journey many secrets which we would probably never share with those who are 'close' to us. This is because we realize when this journey will be over, I am never ever going to meet this person again and whatever opinion he or she might be having about me, what matters is that it can't affect me.

"Oh! How difficult it is to have a good conversation partner these days!," Pankaj often used to think. Having an unguarded conversation is rarity especially at workplaces where colleagues and bosses are always ready to catch you off guard.

Offices have become like chessboards. There you talk and act as if you are making a move thinking what moves people around you are making. Most of the young employees get stuck in honey traps in their first jobs and realise it a little late that how they have been used. So one year down the line, you find most of the young professionals "strategizing" their moves within office. There are groups and lobbies. There are undercover agents who spill the beans about what the other group is doing. It's like war all the time! Who says younger generation hates politics; most of them are completely immersed in politics, only the stage is different. Those who don't like it are dragged into it.

Pankaj looked back at Dr. Tanya. It was like stealing a glance. He could still see her by turning back a little while waiting for the lift to come down. The gym occupied three fourth of the lobby. The entrance to the gym was inside the lobby; the exit was on the other side. In this six storeyed building *"The Daily"* newspaper occupied the rest of the five floors.

The lift was taking too long to come down, so he decided to take the staircase. In three minutes he was at his desk. He placed his note pad, two pens; office ID card on his desk and a shrill ring tone filled the air. It was "Calypso" one of the most common ring tones, quite peppy, but in this office everyone was asked to keep the phone on vibration mode. The Editor hated ring tones as he felt it disturbed journalists who were filing news reports for the day, editing news reports, features or articles or even making pages. So an office order was issued sometime ago which made it mandatory for people to switch their cell phones to vibration mode within office premises.

The ring tone attracted everyone's frown, a few smiled too. The Chief Reporter. Alok Vaidyanathan, had a look of shock. "Whose phone is this,?" Alok got up from his seat as if a tiger gets up and goes for a majestic walk searching for the prey. Pankaj realised the ring tone was coming somewhere from his small carrybag. "How come? I always keep my phone on vibration mode? It cannot be mine." Then he realized his phone was on desk, so it couldn't be his phone.

"It's coming from this," Alok stood in front of Pankaj, pointing a finger at his carrybag. "Please keep your phone on silent mode", It was a natural reaction from Pankaj. "Sir, my phone is here. It's on vibration mode."

Alok was irritated, "But that carrybag is yours. And the ringtone is coming from there Isn't it so?."

"Bloody hell! It must be her phone,"Pankaj fumbled. The frown on Alok's face was getting bigger and bigger. "What the hell? You have your phone and you have another phone in your bag and you don't even know about it. What is happening? Get that phone and shut its mouth before KP (the editor) comes for meeting." Pankaj took the phone out and disconnected the incoming call.

"If you have two mobile phones, keep both of them on vibration or silent mode," Alok barked and went back without waiting to watch how Pankaj had slumped in his chair. He was looking at the phone when it rang suddenly. But Pankaj's reflexes were quick. He could see the screen blinking before the ringtone could take his happiness away and disconnected it.

He took a swig of water from his bottle and called back on the number from which this call had come. It was a landline number. A recorded voice answered back, "This is an information call."

"Damn you!" Pankaj was irritated. Someone doing teleselling had screwed up his day. His mind had started ticking rapidly recounting the events happened on metro. "She must be worried about the phone. Should I wait for her call to come at this number or should I call someone from the address book and tell them to inform the beautiful charming young damsel that she has lost her phone to me and I have probably lost my heart to her…"

Too filmy! Pankaj smiled at himself and put the phone on vibration mode. He was reasoning with himself. "Surfing through the address book would be like invading her privacy, I shouldn't do it. What will she think about me, she might get angry too."?

"Why should I be bothered about her getting angry or not. I should get rid of this phone by handing it over to her. She would have to be infact grateful to me for taking so much pain of surfing through the address book, calling up someone whom she knows and getting the message across to her that I have her cell phone."

His mind was playing games with him.

He didn't realise at that time that it is not only the mind but his fate is also playing games with him. A sweet game, a dangerous game, a nerve wrecking game! He would realise it soon.

"Time for the edit meeting," Sameera nudged him. Pankaj's train of thoughts came to an unscheduled halt. "Oh, when did you come?" he looked at her from his chair.

"I was here, you didn't notice me dear. *Chalo, ab der ho jayegi*, everyone is already in the conference room." He got up and left with a notepad in one hand and two cell phones in the other hand.

"Hey did you get a new mobile phone?" Sameera asked him.

"No, it is not mine." Pankaj said.

"Then whose phone is this?," she sounded surprised even though talking in a low hush-hush voice as they entered the conference room. "It's a long story, I will tell you later," Pankaj said in an even lower voice as they both took their seats as far away from their Chief Reporter as they could.

❑

4

Spreading the Wings

"Oh God!" Her heart skipped too many beats at one go. She had checked her pockets and there was no trace of her mobile phone. "I must have left it in Metro," she cursed herself even while making a desperate attempt to find her mobile phone.

"Oh God, Please, please, please…give back my mobile phone," she silently prayed to the Almighty hoping that she would be able to find the phone in one of her pockets. We all do this when we are desperate. We know we have gone wrong, something wrong has happened which cannot be corrected immediately and yet we pray to God. HE, after all, is the ultimate troubleshooter.

Nisha was not able to find the mobile phone. By the time her frantic search had ended, she had reached Kasturba Gandhi Marg. Her brisk walk went unnoticed as at that time of the hour, there were already too many people walking at a faster pace than her. Droplets of sweat started appearing on her forehead. Some of them were apparently due to hot weather and some due to the realization that she had lost her mobile phone. It was the latest model of Nokia and she had paid Rs 12,000 in cash for that. At 21, it is not a small amount especially if you have spent almost same amount of money twice in the last six months. She had lost a mobile phone within weeks of buying it and then her elder brother had bought her another one.

Nisha tried to calm herself. She couldn't afford to look disturbed right now. This was her first job interview. She looked at the building in front of her. To read the name of the building written at the top she had to tilt her head back. "Yes, this is it," she almost whispered to herself.

She looked at her watch, it was exactly five minutes to twelve. She had just reached in time for the interview. Even as she checked whether all the documents were in place, she was telling herself, "Grrr……I am angry, damn angry with myself but I will have to manage it for the time being." She wanted to kill herself for losing the cell phone.

She told herself, "The first thing I have to do is to block my sim card.," hoping that someone who got hold of the sim card wouldn't misuse it much for the next hour or so.

"I will do it after the interview," she reminded herself.

She once again checked the folder and rushed into the building. Fortunately for her, the place where she had to go to the interview was on the ground floor.

First interview is like first love for a middle class youngster. You don't know what is going to happen to you, the only thing you realise is that you may be in deep shit and so deep that you may not be able to come out of it unscathing. Some stink, some have scars after this experience. But with passage of time these scars heal, though they do leave their mark more than often.

She rushed to the reception where a young lady was sitting behind a huge desk.

"Hi, I am Nisha, I have come for the interview," she fumbled while informing the receptionist.

"For which post? There are lot of interviews lined up today?"

"For the post of Assistant Sales Manager."

"Ok. Wait."

Nisha collapsed into a sofa chair which was kept on left side of reception desk. Her best friend Lata's face flashed in front of her. She had told her once, "First love and first interview have one thing in common. They often excite you too much as you think you are going to be on the top of the world and most of the time you come crashing down. And even those who succeed often realise a few months (if they are lucky enough) and few years (if they still remain sane enough) later that how stupid they were."

Lata's thoughts were like guided missiles. She practiced to hit the targets with all and sundry. Nisha was one of the best practicing fields she had got. Both of them had met in college and jelled together well. After graduation from Kalindi College in Delhi University, both of them did a two-year MBA from Indraprastha University, Delhi.

Their results had come out a couple of months ago. They were not picked up in Campus interviews. "The reason was that there were no campus interviews!," Lata had told her parents who lived in Patna after they called her forcing her to come back and get married to son of a local contractor after they came to know that she hasn't been able to get a job even after doing MBA.

Nisha too had given the same reply to her father in Chandigarh. Her father had told her on phone, "Listen, you should come back here. I have lot of contacts. I will get you a job in any of the corporate companies here." Nisha kept listening. She had stopped arguing with her father long ago.

"There is no point in arguing with your parents. They would win ultimately. They will resort to all kinds of tricks – threat, anger and worst of all emotional blackmail.Fathers would pretend to fall sick, mothers would become crying machines making life hell for all those youngsters who want to spread their wings and test new horizons," Lata would say frustratingly.

Nisha knew, how Lata's parents were ready to bear the mediocrity of their son who had failed in civil services examination twice. But they were always pushing Lata to just get married and get off their backs.

"Mohali (a suburb near Chandigarh) has all the top companies. My friends' sons and daughters are all working there.

I got these jobs for many of them. Why wouldn't I do it for you. Infact, I will get you the best possible job, much better in profile and salary than all your friends with whom you studied," Nisha's father told her after she informed him that she would have to search out for a job on her own in Delhi as the promise of "campus interviews" mentioned in the glamourous brochure of their institute did not materialise.

The more her father, like any other Indian middle class father, was trying to convince her, the more bitter she was getting on phone. Everyone has many unforgettable moments during life. She, unlike others, probably had more than few. Though it is a different matter that most of us feel the same way! Ironically most of us feel that others are living a much happier life than us.

Nisha wanted to say something bluntly to her father during all these conversations but then didn't. Something inside her made her keep quiet. It was not respect but something else. What it was, she didn't know. She didn't even want to find out. There are certain feelings which can't be defined. They should be allowed to remain as they are, there is no other way out. Let them be.

Talking to her father even on phone often left her exhausted, she couldn't understand why. Her friends in college often used to talk so fondly about their fathers. But she didn't. Somehow she couldn't relate to him the way many of her friends felt close to their fathers.

Anyone would have expected that a girl, who is not close to her father must be close to her mother. But even that was not the case to be.

Why this happened? "I don't know," she told herself several times. It was probably the fallout of a sacred relationship she had seen going haywire. Everything was fine till she reached Class VIII. Her father was doing well. She had an elder brother. They were living in a relatively smaller house in Chandigarh in Sector-10. It was single storeyed house but there was enough space for everyone.

But then things started turning upside down. These are the ways of the world, she realised years later, but little did an VIII class student knew that life could be nasty to kids too. It doesn't matter how old you are, life doesn't differentiate between the young and the old, it flows like a flooded river refusing to pay any heed to feelings, washing off everything in swift strokes.

Her father also didn't understand this though he realized that somewhere, somehow the string of affection between the two just did not exist anymore. Nisha wished he could. But he couldn't. He was a senior officer in Chandigarh Administration. He had done reasonably well in life though he had struggled hard too.

She studied in Chandigarh till she finished her school. But then moved to Delhi on pretext of higher studies. She just wanted to get away from her father. It was suffocating there for her. Her father reminded her of the betrayal her mother had faced at his hands. Her mother was close to her during her school days.

Memories came back to her in flashes though, it shouldn't have been happening right now. But has anyone ever been able to control the memories? They haunt you when you want to get away from them. They are like shadows, the follow you, confront you and many a times they walk just quietly with you.

They are as mysterious as the first rain after summers which creates an aroma all around you and leaves a lingering feeling which persists for a much longer duration than the rain itself.

The train of memories came to a halt as an exhausted Nisha heard a voice from a little distance, "Nisha, Please go straight, turn left at the end of the corridor and there would be a room on the left hand side at the end of corridor. You will be interviewed there. The CEO and GM (Sales) will take your interview."

Nisha had no time to even realise the fact that the voice of this girl who was informing her sounded more like a pre-recorded promotional voice messages on mobile phones. All such voices sound similar and all of them irritate equally.

She gathered herself, clutched her file tightly in her hands, with her right hand pulled back a few strands of hair which had the tenacity to slip quietly from her head to her forehead and swiftly got up from the sofa with a sense of mission. She hurriedly started walking in a brightly lit corridor.

She took less than a minute and found herself standing in front of a closed door. In that fraction of a minute she tried to memorise all the sermons in self-help books which she had read over the last few years. They give you so many tips to be successful. But unfortunately she couldn't remember anything.

"What the heck, *jo hoga dekha jayega*," this was the last thought in her mind as she knocked on the door with a light green-paint on it. A small brass plate at the centre of the door informed—"General Manager (Sales)."

"Hello sir, I am Nisha," she entered the room after knocking and said this much rehearsed one-liner with all the courage she could muster. A 35-year-old balding man wearing a colourful shirt was sitting behind a desk. Along with him was another gentleman who looked around 45-years-old. The former was the GM (Sales) of YOUR GYM, Anurag Chopra while the latter was the owner Sudhir Yadav.

Chopra welcomed her with a smile and indicated her to sit in a chair across the desk. Yadav had an expressionless face. They already had her CV in front of them.

"So why do you want to join our organization and what value you can bring to us?," Chopra fired the first salvo.

The most common question asked in interviews, yet the most difficult one to answer.

Probably, the fact is that at the lower and middle level it has become a ritual to begin an interview with this question. Though most of the times the answer doesn't have much bearing on selection of the candidate.

Nisha took the salvo in her stride and launched a counter-offensive, "Sir, YOUR GYM is a fast-growing chain of heatlh and fitness clubs and it would be a great opportunity for a fresher like me to be a part of this growing organization."

"As far as bringing value is concerned, I am an MBA with specialization in sales and marketing. I am hardworking and ready to learn. I am a team player…" That's it. She had rehearsed to say so many other things about her qualities during the mock interview sessions she had with Lata after she got this interview call. Everything vaporized.

"But you have no experience, how will you handle sales here," Chopra's second salvo.

This is another common technique of assault by an interviewer. But the candidate has to adopt guerrilla tactics. Take one step back and then launch a full-blown counter offensive. Nisha did exactly the same thing.

She took one step back, "You are right Sir, I have no experience."

Chopra was gleeful though he tried to hide this feeling that overtake interviewers when they are able to make the life of the candidate, who is interviewed, miserable.

But he didn't realise the gusto with which this young woman was going to take the bull by horns. Nisha took a not-so-deep breath and opened fire, "But Sir what I don't have in terms of experience, I have in terms of determination, skill sets, academic qualifications and an urge and will to succeed and do my organization proud."

As words started coming towards Chopra like bullets, though Nisha was talking very politely, Chopra was groping for a more lethal weapon from his armoury of questions.

Meanwhile, Yadav continued to sit expressionless. Questions kept on coming from Chopra for next 30 minutes. Nisha tried to answer all of them as best as she could. At the end of 30 minutes, Chopra told her, "Ok, Nisha you can go now, We will get back to you."

❑

5

Jab they Met

Pankaj was watching news on television which was tucked away in a corner of reporting room. He didn't have an assignment for the day. Probably he would make a few phone calls to check whether anything interesting was happening.

The reporting room was half empty. Sameera had gone to attend a press conference in Hotel Shangri-la at Ashoka Road a couple of kilometers away from his office. She would be back by 4.30 p.m. It was relatively a lean day. No major accidents in the city so far. No CBI raids, traffic was normally stuck at most of the places and extended beyond a couple of miles on MG road, Vikas Marg, ITO. The roads were busy, Jantar Mantar did not have any major demonstration. Ramlila Maidan was also sitting empty, looking at Turkman Gate in the neighbourhood. All in all, the major news-spots were cool on this day. So far, so good. You never know when a bomb would explode, a luxury car would crush a family or suddenly some big political leader would die.

Another loud ring. "Calypso" started playing on the mobile phone again which was neatly put along with his phone at his desk. This was the phone that beautiful young woman had forgotten in the Metro. Pankaj picked up the phone. "Hello, This is Pankaj, may I know who is on the line." A female voice on the other end, "Mr Pankaj, I had forgotten this phone somewhere today, may be in the Metro, I hope I can come and collect it from you."

Pankaj stammered a little bit, "Oh… yes,..no— I mean yes, yes, sure." He wanted to tell her, how good he felt that she had called up even though it was on her own phone. He didn't realize that just less than 10 metres away from his building she heaved a sigh of relief as soon as he had answered the call. She was visibly relaxed now and managed to focus on the lemonade she was sipping while standing at Kasturba Gandhi Marg's only public telephone booth which was functional, courtesy the telephone department.

Nisha was thinking, "Thank God, you heard my prayers. My mobile phone is with someone who is going to return it to me."

"Where can I collect it, can you give me your address," she said hoping that the person should be in CP (Connaught Place) itself and not at some far end of Delhi.

Pankaj's mind started racing. He didn't want to invite her to his office. "Tongues will start wagging. Moreover his boss didn't like friends or relatives coming to meet staffers during the day for any personal work."

"Mr. Pankaj, are you there?," the female voice buzzed from the phone.

Pankaj again stammered, "Yes, yes, I am there… and then without giving it much thought he blurted spontaneously," Look I am not in my office right now but in half an hour or so I would be at the Rajiv Chowk Metro Station. Can you come there?"

Nisha was even more relieved. She didn't want to go to any stranger's office. A public place is much safer. She said, "Ok, but how do I recognize you and where would I meet you?"

"You can take my mobile number and I would be standing in front of the Nirula's outlet there. It is 2 p.m. right now. I would be there at 2.30 p.m."

"Thanks a lot, I would be there at 2.30 p.m.," Nisha said after scribbling down a cell number on a piece of paper which was actually a tissue paper that she had picked up at the gym where she had given an interview few moments ago.

Pankaj was not sure whether he has done the right thing by calling her to Rajiv Chowk Metro Station. It is the biggest Metro Station in Delhi, a hub from where regular travellers change metros to travel in different directions.

It is a sprawling place with thousands of travellers boarding and getting down from trains almost every second minute. Wisely, the Delhi Metro Rail Corporation has been able to exploit its commercial potential with several major brands opening their outlets there which makes it an ideal rendezvous for friends, lovers, and siblings alike.

So much has been its popularity as a meeting place that it has infact become a major dating hub. where else the young teenagers can meet in an air conditioned environment without spending a single penny if they don't want to. They can eat, have coffee, buy books and DVDs as gifts for each other here.

And if it is the end of the month with the guys having nowehere to turn to for borrowing money as their friends have also exhausted their pocket money, they can always sit at the stairs at the entry and exit gates of the station. It is much safer to meet there for youngsters than many other crowded places.

One generally finds college students or teenagers sitting there. They can find some peace here as in this city everyone stares at a young man and woman sitting too close for their comfort, especially if the latter doesn't have a sprinkle of vermillion on her forehead declaring that she is married. Officially!

"So be it," Pankaj told himself trying to reason whether he took the right decision by calling this young female to the Rajiv Chowk Metro Station. He shook his head, "*Itna Sochna Kya Hai Yaar*," he told himself.

But mind plays games all the times. It doesn't allow you to rest. "I could have met her downstairs or in a nearby restaurant.

There are several coffee joints in the outer periphery of Connaught Place, on the way to Rajiv Chowk Metro Station."

"But why would she come to a coffee joint? Wouldn't she think that I am trying to explore the chance of having an affair with her? Isn't calling a girl for coffee too clichéd?," a part of his mind was trying to confuse him.

Another part of his mind sheepishly smiled, "Don't give this crap. Of all the places, you called her to the Metro Station. You would walk down all the way there to handover a mobile phone. Are you not trying to court her? Don't you like her? Wouldn't you like to go around with her and explore further possibilities?"

Pankaj was getting restless. He went out of the office and bought a cigarette from the nearby kiosk. "Look what she is doing to you, you generally don't smoke and here you have just talked to this girl once and you have been thrown off balance? You seem to be falling in love with this girl," the mind games started again.

Pankaj was tired of these trains of conflicting thoughts which kept on ramming into each other as he started his brisk walk towards the Rajiv Chowk Metro Station. It was 2.10 p.m.

He didn't realise that the girl he is going to meet in next half an hour is going to be a part of the same milieu of people which seemed to be moving in all directions. A crowd moves like a crowd, there is no set pattern. There is no method to the madness especially when a crowd is moving at a Metro Station on Delhi. One can feel that it is not moving anywhere and one can also feel at the same time that it is moving too fast.

Nisha was walking briskly too. She had her handbag on one shoulder. It was a fake Louis Vuitton. Even the monogram was there. Nisha had bought it last year from a local handbag shop in Karol Bagh. She had liked the design, it made her poorer by around Rs. 1000. The original Louis Vuitton of same make would have made her much more poorer.

She continued to swipe her forehead with a bunch of tissues clutched in her right hand. It was hot and humid and she was feeling a little feverish too. She was feeling that her stomach is cramped hardly realizing that it has less to do with the scorching sun. She had missed her breakfast as usual.

That is typical of a single person who lives in Delhi, especially the youngsters. Most of them miss their breakfast. It's natural. "Who the hell wants to get up and cook when one is getting late for the college classes or their high-pressure jobs." So the routine is very common and similar for most of the undergraduate students living in Delhi, "Get up late, take a bath, if you can afford then have a cup of tea or probably finish the half empty bottle of pepsi which was left last night on the table along with crumbs of Pizza strewn within the cardboard case, sent by the local Pizza joint at your doorstep in the late evening.

Then one had a late night chat session with the friends – it could be face-to-face, on SMS or on Internet. Whatever it was, it left you exhausted and you slept at 3 a.m., it was still early. The night before that, it had extended to five in the morning. The class is at 10 or you have to reach office by 9:30 in morning, so you have to leave the house at 8:30 a.m. to catch the nearest Metro or a bus. The alarm clock kept on ringing but no one heard it and you got up late at 7.45 a.m. giving you just enough time to brush your teeth, have a quick shower and change of clothes. You have to locate your watch, wallet, mobile, earphones, hand sanitizer and the bag.

You manage to leave the house in time only because breakfast does not figure in the list of priorities early morning. You can always grab a sandwich from one of the outlets opened at several Metro Stations and munch it while gulping down Diet Coke.

Nisha was no exception. Though she and Lata stayed together. But both of them often skipped cooking. Lata's favourite line, on most of the evenings was, "*Saari zindagi yahi to karna hai, abhi to relax kar yaar nisha, Just chill na.*"

So with a cramped up stomach Nisha continued to walk briskly towards the Rajiv Chowk Metro Station. Now, after a hectic couple of hours, during which she lost her phone, was interviewed for the job of an Assistant Sales Manager in a gym and was able to get hold of the guy who had her cell phone, she was moving towards the Metro Station.

The schedule for the rest of the day was clear. She will take her cell phone from this guy who is going to meet her at the metro station in next few minutes. Then she will catch a metro back to Patel Nagar. From Rajiv Chowk it would take her around 15-20 minutes to reach Patel Nagar Station. From there she would take a cycle-rickshaw and reach her rented accommodation in another 10 minutes.

Then she would take a shower, eat something and watch a movie on her laptop. Nisha continued to walk. It was blistering heat but she didn't care. She was used to it. Delhi is a city which ensures you get adapted to extreme weather faster than you expect. The rule for survival is simple—Adapt or Perish. You will curse, get nostalgic about your home town but you would live in Delhi. It gets under your skin.

As she walked towards the station and reached near one of the famous restaurants 'Blue Legend', it reminded her of the good time she had here with her friends. They used to come here for celebrating birthdays of their friends. The "Footlong" here was her favourite. Her friends rather found shots of Vodka more exciting.

The joint became her favourite and one particular incident cemented this loyalty further. It was about an year back. They had come here, a group of five students, to celebrate Malini's birthday.

They were sitting around second table on the left row. The air conditioning was most effective here so it had become their favourite table. Frequent visits to some particular restaurants always ensure that you would know of the corners where you could sit more comfortably, quietly without noise and enjoy your meals.

Then this young couple walked in with a kid who seemed to be around five years old. There was a twinkle in his eye and he insisted that while the mother waited at a corner table meant for four, he would accompany his father to the self-service counter where the father was picking up two trays having burgers, French fries and two large glasses of coke.

As they were walking back to the table, the child slipped and in a sudden reflex tried to catch hold of his father. The latter lost balance and both the trays came crashing down on the floor. Everything was spilled on the floor.

The father unlike many others did not scold the child and was instead helping him to get up and telling him, "Don't worry son, we will order food again." The child still seemed petrified. The mother came rushing down to see that her child was not injured and before she could say anything the father was telling her, "Don't scold the child, it happens. I will order the food again." Others in the restaurant had started eating their food again while a couple of staffers came to clean the floor.

Meanwhile, a young chap came. A small brass plate tucked on his shirt was shining with "Assistant Manager" written on it. He put his hand on the child's head and asked him, "Hey! Are you OK? I hope you are not hurt." The father said, "Sorry for the mess, the child slipped."

The Assistant Manager with a million dollar smile said, "No problem, Sir. We will bring your order on the table itself." The father said, "I will just pay at the billing counter." But before he could turn back to move towards the billing counter, the young Assistant Manager with a million dollar smile said, "Please Sir, you don't have to pay again. Kindly take your seat. We would get the order."

Within minutes the order had reached their table and the three—father, mother and the son started enjoying their meals. Nisha was overwhelmed. "It doesn't happen in cities like this.

That incident was etched in her memory forever." After all how many times you come across such incidents and that too in a city like Delhi or as a matter of fact in any other city.

Every time she was near Blue Legend, this incident made her smile. She took a deep breath and continued walking. The mercury was rising but that couldn't deter her from walking at a brisk pace.

She entered the Rajiv Chowk Metro Station and opted for stairs instead of an escalator. During afternoon hours, you could atleast enter the metro station at Rajiv Chowk without getting pushed. In 45 seconds she had covered the stairs and in next 30 seconds she reached at the security check point. She checked, as a habit, in her back pocket whether her metro travelling pass commonly as well as officially known as "Smart Card" was there.

She went through the security check behind a make shift closure where a woman cop from Central Industry Security Force, a para-military organization of the Indian government, checked her physically with bare hands.

She moved ahead and passed her file folder through the security machine. The cop sitting on one side of the machine was able to watch contents of all the bags passing through the machine on a computer screen. He was sitting nonchalantly.

Nisha moved ahead, reached the entrance and touched her smart card at designated spot on the mechanized entrance which opened and allowed her to pass through it.

She walked about five meters and then turned to her right. There was Nirula's, a popular eating outlet. A clean-shaven guy, five feet seven inches in height with a medium built was visible. "This could be the person I am supposed to meet for my phone." While thinking this she moved towards the outlet.

She was hesitant and this was reflected in her movements and her voice which almost dropped to the non-audible level, "Excuse me, are you the person who I am supposed to meet here to take back my mobile phone." This was a funny expression but what else she could say though she would laugh about it later on more than one occasion.

There was a billboard blinking latest advertisement of a product behind Nisha which she could not see. Pankaj, however, glanced at the tag line - "Life is full of surprises!"

❑

6

Smitten!

Pankaj was watching blankly at the computer screen in front of him. Two hours earlier a hurricane had hit him. The name of this hurricane was "Nisha." He was smitten by her charm but found it ridiculous that it happened to him.

While handing over the mobile phone to her in the middle of a massive crowd, he didn't feel anything.

"Thanks a lot for coming all the way to hand over the phone," Nisha had told him. He was slightly embarrassed and didn't know where to go with his modesty. He could just stammer, "It's OK."

They exchanged the usual pleasantries. So many questions were popping up on his mind's screen. But only three things registered in his mind finally. First, her name was Nisha. Second, she had lost her cell phone in the Metro train. And third, she was very happy to get back her phone.

This hurricane stayed around him for around six minutes. He had told her, "I am Pankaj." And without even being asked he told her that he was journalist and had an office on Kasturba Gandhi Marg from where he had walked down to hand over the phone.

Both of them had repeated the clichéd parting off shot, "Nice meeting you." And parted off. Pankaj, though wanted to say, "See you again soon."

While walking back from the Metro Station, he received a few calls and didn't get time to realize the impact of meeting a simple girl. But now a couple of hours later, he was finding it difficult to concentrate on work.

It was around 5.30 p.m. Time to start punching keys to churn out a few hundred words for tomorrow's newspapers. He hadn't got any story listed today.

He just couldn't stop thinking about her. Her eyes, her face and the warmth of her hand when they shook hands before parting. He didn't remember who extended the hand first he himself or her.

There was a tap on his shoulder, "You haven't listed any story today. Alok will kill you. There are no advertisements on city pages and at least three reporters are on leave. So we have to fill these pages."

She took a deep breath and continued, "There will be no evening edit meeting today but Alok has asked me to compile the list of stories and give it to him. Raman has listed three, Anusha listed two, Ragini three. There will be three or four copies from the court reporters and a few late night press releases from Delhi Police will be helpful but there is no major government story."

Pankaj turned towards Sameera. And she stopped. She looked at him and smiled, "Did you meet someone today dude? What happened? Got an offer letter with a hike and promotion from our rival newspaper?"

Now he was getting irritated. He told himself, "What the hell? Why can't she stop chattering?" Sameera dragged a chair and asked him again. "Hey Pankaj! are you OK?"

Pankaj managed to answer, "Yeah, I am fine."

Coming back to the real world, he asked, "What were you saying?" Sameera inhaled a deep breath and then said, "So you didn't listen to what I was telling you just now?"

Sameera was wondering what has happened to this guy. She had never seen him like this.

She was staring at his face. Around 10 kms away oblivious from this exchange of strange looks, Nisha was humming an old Hindi film song as her laptop played the same. In between, she was taking swigs of Pepsi, trying to clean her cupboard and thinking aloud, "What to cook for this evening?"

She didn't know why but she felt good and her spirits were elevated. The interview had gone well, she had been able to find her mobile phone even after losing it and after a long long time she had met a decent guy.

A bolt from the blue hit her.

"Why should she be thinking about this guy who returned her cell phone.?"

"Why not?," the other half of her mind said. She had met enough number of guys who just couldn't take their eyes off her body as she cringed and wanted to run away somewhere. They were all over—in college, metro, buses, multiplexes and even in the bylanes she crossed everyday to reach the Metro Station and back home.

"Don't get too judgemental, you met her only for four minutes," she told herself.

The chain of thoughts was broken by a shrill tone. It took her a few seconds to realize that it was her mobile phone. She pressed the green button on it and a voice boomed from other side. "Hi, How was your interview. *Baat bani kya?*".

It was Lata. Nisha didn't respond. She didn't know how to respond. She didn't know what to say. Later on when would analyse these moments she would find it funny to be standing dazed like this.

Lata again shouted, "Are you listening Nisha? *Kya hua, sab theek hai na*?"

"Oh, I am fine. ...When are you coming back?"

Lata said, "I am going to start in a few minutes from here. I should reach in one and a half hour maximum."

"OK, Comeback, then we will talk.. ..."

"By the way what are you cooking?"

"I don't know, probably some *khichdi*..."

There was a silence on other side and then almost an order, “Sweetheart don’t cook anything, we will order a Pizza. Bye.”

Before Nisha could refute this suggestion, the phone was disconnected.

It was twice a week ritual by now. Nisha wanted to save money and preferred to cook at their two-room accommodation while Lata loved to order Pizzas.

Both of them had been staying together in Patel Nagar for almost two years. They had changed their accommodation twice. Certain things remained common however—shortage of water, exorbitant rent, men and boys in the neighbourhood trying to be extra helpful and the once a fortnight argument between Lata and Nisha.

While Nisha wanted to keep their house clean with whatever furniture they had, Lata had a different take on such efforts, “*Arey yaar ghar thode na basana hai yahan.*”

But Nisha had somehow, probably an inkling that it is going to be a long stay here in this city. Much longer than probably even she wanted. In fact she had started enjoying her solitude. It was no more loneliness for her.

So she would keep the house clean, wash clothes, take off dust from the furniture—“two folding cots, a small wooden cupboard, a small table and three chairs.”

She would diligently water the plants. She had even given them names. It all started when Lata and Nisha were sitting together talking about endless number of things. So while one of the plants was named, “Luck”, the other one was “Smiley.”, the rest of them were named after their favourite Bollywood actors—Amitabh, Shahrukh, Akshay, Kareena and Katrina. In all they were seven, lucky seven.

They ensured that while changing houses all the ‘lucky seven’ travelled with them and were taken care of very well. Nisha would sometime sit near them and could feel she could talk to them. She didn’t tell this Lata as she felt this could be too much for her to handle but she always felt comfortable whenever she was around Luck, Smiley, Amitabh, Shahrukh, Akshay, Kareena and Katrina.

Pankaj was ferociously punching the keyboard. He had finally got hold of couple of decent stories on phone. There was an important meeting of the heads of civic agencies in Delhi to take decision about construction of half a dozen new flyovers. One of his sources had given him enough information to churn out a decent 350 word story which could be used as a lead item for the city page.

He had to finish it by 7.30 p.m. so that it could go the early city edition which was printed by midnight and sent for distribution to some of the nearby towns in Delhi. He was left with only half an hour. During the last one hour, he had finally agreed to tell nagging Sameera that something had happened during the day which left him dazed. They had decided to talk about it while walking down to Rajiv Chowk Metro Station after work.

From there Pankaj would take the Metro going towards Dwarka while Sameera would take Metro which travels towards the Delhi University's North Campus. She was staying in a Paying Guest (PG) accommodation at Mukherjee Nagar. It was a ten minutes ride on rickshaw from the nearest metro station to her house.

Most of the days they would walk to the metro station together and talk about life, office, home, problems, solutions, frustrations, happiness—all that constituted their day-to-day life. The only days when they could not walk together were when Pankaj went to the Press Club for a drink or when either of them got stuck in office due to some story.

Sameera was looking at her computer screen with the concentration of a hunter chasing the prey. In the newsroom, half a dozen reporters were punching their keyboards. The most prominent sound in the newsrooms which appear like symphony to journalists is "Tik, Tik, Tik…." coming from the keyboards of the reporters who try to meet the tight deadlines everyday.

There were empty cups of tea on desks, two reporters had potato chips packs lying unattended. While filing a story reporters often lose touch with their immediate surroundings. The words blinking on their screens are all that matter to them.

Alok was sitting in his cubicle looking at some important stories, checking flow of stories from news agencies which kept on appearing in a customised format. He was assigning some of them to the reporters. They were the ones which needed to be followed by them.

The sound of keys being punched was getting more and more rhythmic as the deadline for submitting stories was approaching.

Pankaj keyed in the final line of the story, ran a quick spell check, checked the tentative headline and punched the final key which transferred the story to the desk for editing. Immediately after that he took a deep breath, exhaled it with full force and leaned back a little on chair. That was his natural reaction after filing an important story.

He got up to stretch himself a little bit. More work was to be done. There were a couple of routine press releases which were to be filed in as brief news items so that if needed they could be used as single-column stories to fill up the page. It was another half-an-hour job for him.

Both of them—Sameera and Pankaj—almost finished their work simultaneously at around 8.30 p.m. He was behaving normally now as he moved to Sameera's terminal and told her, " I am done. What about you?"

"I am almost done. Wait for five minutes."

❑

7

Flying without Wings

Is it love? May be, may be not. He didn't know. He couldn't ask. He wanted to ask someone but knew there was no perfect answer for this.

It was sweltering heat outside. Pankaj entered the main gate of his office building at 11.30 a.m. sharp. He stopped before entering the lobby and took a deep breath. "May be, I can meet her today, or at least see her?" He looked from across the glass door. The same old receptionist *errr*...Dr. Soumya was sitting there. She had stopped looking beautiful to him ever since he had met Nisha. Even though it was a momentary meeting but it turned out to be a momentous one for him.

It had been three days since he got that interesting call. He was sitting at his chair, waiting for a phone call from a source who had told him that morning that he had some interesting documents related to a scam in the Municipal Corporation of Delhi's Engineering Department.

Pankaj was excited and he had forgotten the fact he had not been able to sleep for a couple of days atleast. If he remembered correctly, he had handed over the mobile phone to this sweet looking girl with an innocent face on June 23. Pankaj was bad at keeping records of dates but he somehow could not forget this one.

What compounded his agony was the fact that he was not able to take this girl out of his mind. He told himself, "It is ridiculous. It can't happen like this, not with me. I just met her for few minutes. How can I not forget her?"

"Leave aside forgetting what is there to remember?"

These arguments were of no use.

His agony continued to grew. The day he had met her, he was dazed. He tried to share what happened during the day with Sameera later when they went to catch the Metro in late evening but could not. Somehow he didn't feel like talking about this to anyone.

It continued to get more ridiculous. On 24 June, he forgot his telephone diary at one of the press conference he had gone to attend. He was aghast to know that he had forgotten it.

But what could he do. This sweet, innocent girl to whom he had handed over her mobile had dominated his thoughts so much that his friends had to nudge him to move towards exit gate after the press conference was over.

Probably he had kept his telephone diary at the chair next to him or it just slipped from his pocket. It was a small pocket diary but for a journalist, "Telephone Diary" is the most precious thing. They guard it with ferocity of the most dangerous warrior. This is the magic box which they open as they search for dope on anyone.

Legend is that many a journalists reached at the top because of the telephone diaries! The thickness of a telephone diary often betrays how deeply entrenched a journalist is in terms of his or her network of sources and resources.

Though many young journalists save numbers in the phonebook of the cell phones and do not carry the traditional telephone diaries anymore in their pockets. But still as they grow older they realize that some numbers cannot be saved in mobile. Generally they are contact numbers of top level sources. "Top sources" or "Highly Placed Sources" as they are quoted in news reports are generally senior bureaucrats and senior politicians who provide information to journalists.

It takes years to build these contacts. The details of such contacts are generally kept hidden in telephone diaries which are kept locked safely in office drawers or at home with an additional copy. Most of the journalists remember many of these phone numbers and they do not have to look into the diary to call them.

They will not share these contact details with anyone—not even God leave aside the family, friends or their colleagues.

There was no end to Pankaj's misery thus as he had lost his 'precious' telephone diary. He was fortunate enough that one of the executives of the public relations firm which handled this press conference knew him well, so she came in the evening to his office to hand over him the diary.

Before Pankaj could pour out his heart to thank her profusely for all the pain she took to come all the way to his office, she quietly slipped a press release from another of her client with a cheesy smile. "Could you please put a few lines on this too?" Pankaj looked at her and then his telephone diary and was reminded of Sameera's favourite one-liner, "There are no free lunches in life! So look before you leap and think before you speak."

He decided not to respond for a moment and then with a deep breath decided to pay for his own sins. "OK! I will try but there is not much space on page. But still I will try."

The executive widened her cheesy smile which she had never taken off during this two and a half minute conversation. "Thanks a lot. I will give you a call tomorrow. Please let me know if it gets published."

That simply meant, "I am not going to let you live in peace until you carry this item as I am not a bloody fool that I came all the way to hand you over this diary. It's pay back time."

Pankaj took another deep breath. He was getting irritated but he could not afford. He was a gentleman and knew that had it not been for this PR executive, this could have been a major setback for his career, atleast momentarily, as one can't tell one's boss, "I missed that story yesterday because I have lost contact details of my sources as I lost my telephone diary in a press conference."

Pankaj's miserable life continued for another three days. And then on 28 June, Monday, he received a phone call on his cell phone.

He had just got into the Metro at around 11 a.m. from Rajouri Garden Metro Station. He entered the third coach. The crowd was there but it was not a mob. During peak hours in morning and evening when officegoers take Metro, the crowd turns into a mob. People fight, children cry, women take sighs and people just push each other till they reach their station.

Travellers during these hours behave as if taking a seat or standing in a preferred corner is like matter of life and death. Pankaj used to think, "How can they behave in such a manner? Executives with smart ties and even smarter shirts and trousers are as rowdy as the 'babus' working in various government offices in and around the Metro route. Atleast fifty per cent of them get down at Rajiv Chowk and their average travel time from their point of boarding to the destination would be around half-an-hour.

But during that half-an-hour they can give any Bollywood scriptwriter run for their money. They are sarcasm personified. Their tongue lashings are as wild as jungle fires and they spread too like jungle fires. Once, one of the travellers start tongue lashing the other one, it soon turns into a slanging match.

Those who do not participate in this slang contest, they behave like dodos. "Robots, listening the music!"

Pankaj had just kept down his bag and was going to take out the water flask to take a swig of water. It was humid and his shirt was drenched with sweat. He wish he could wear a Tee-Shirt everyday to office but the unwritten rule in his office was to wear Tee-Shirts and Jeans only on weekends. During the week he needed to wear casual trousers and casual shirts with shoes. Informal wear was allowed on weekends.

Before entering the profession, he had thought journalists, especially reporters could wear anything at office except shorts. But little did he realize that the days of *kurta-payjama* and a "*jhola*"(a cotton handbag with a long sling) were over.

Newspapers are now products. Brand Managers wield more power than editors and corporate culture has swept every nook and corner of the newsrooms.

There was a buzz and vibration in his shirt pocket. There was a call. He saw the number and couldn't recognize it. Unlike many others reporters take calls from all kind of numbers. They do not have a choice as one doesn't know which call could turn out to be the one giving them a lifetime story. Though no one remembers when was the last time a phone call to journalist's cell had changed his life professionally catapulting him into a big league but the tradition continues.

So Pankaj picked up the phone.

It was 28 June, 11.05 a.m.

"Hello"

"Hello Mr. Pankaj, Is it a good time to talk to you?"

Pankaj recognized the voice faintly. He had heard it recently.

Before he could tell her that this was the worst time to talk to him as he was soaking in sweat trying to get some air conditioning in metro and was being pushed and nudged by one of his burly fellow traveller who just couldn't stand still, the voice boomed again, "Are you there Mr. Pankaj?"

He thought in an instant, "Goddamn it! Another telecaller."

He was a in a mood to cut the call curtly by pressing on the red button on his phone when something stopped him. He was listening to her trying to place the voice in his brain's blackbox. "Where the hell I have listened to this voice?"

He missed out on what this girl was telling him.

"Mr Pankaj, I am calling from 'Your GYM', We have a corporate tie-up with your office where employees from your organization get 50 per cent off on annual membership fee. Many of your colleagues have already registered with us. I would request you to take a look at the gym and spend a couple of hours for next few days according to your convenience. ...”

She was blurting out all the details, all the packages, all the offers this gym had at a speed which could give any bullet train a run for its money.

Pankaj was listening to her but nothing registered in his mind. Three minutes had passed. The train suddenly stopped with a jolt between Moti Nagar and Kirti Nagar Metro Stations. And the recorded message played on the public address system in the metro, “There will be a short delay…”

Pankaj was pushed out of his stupor. He suddenly realized, this the voice of the girl who had made his life miserable during last five days. His hands shook a little bit. He was suddenly feeling a little feverish, stunned, startled and at loss of words.

“Mr. Pankaj, we also have spa and sauna. The members can use this facility anytime. The access is unrestricted.”

Then in a flash of moment, Pankaj gripped his phone so tightly that his fingers ached and asked, “Hey wait! Had you lost your mobile phone a few days ago in Metro and someone handed over you the mobile phone.....”

Pankaj waited with baited breath for the reply and then suddenly realized, the call had got disconnected. It was network problem. Pankaj wanted to smash his phone for a moment. He was telling himself, “I wanted to talk to her. That was my only chance of meeting her. May be, may be…this was going to click…”.

He could only mumble to himself, “Damn it!”

The metro started moving.

11.12 a.m.

He checked his watch. A lifetime has gone by it seemed.

Then in a flash of a second an idea hit him. He decided to check the number from which this call had come. “May be I can call back and find out who was talking to me.” Though he knew the probability to succeed in this kind of investigation was abysmally low.

"But atleast I have a lead to work on, what kind of a journalist I am if I cannot locate this woman who called me." He looked at the phone screen, pressed the button and went to "menu", selected the option "Received Calls", held his breath and pressed the button with a shaking thumb.

On the top of the list of "received calls" was an entry. He looked at it and his heart skipped a beat. It read.

"Unknown Number"

"Godaaamn it ..." he cursed the mobile phone network which went down at just the "right" time.

His train of thoughts was broken as the metro screeched to a halt with a slight jerk and the public address system said, "This is Rajiv Chowk Metro Station". People pushed each other to get outside. Those who were standing outside were pushing to come inside.

It is a funny scene every time a metro stops at the Rajiv Chowk Metro Station. There is always a long queue of people standing to board the train.

However, as soon as the Metro stops, the queue vanishes and people appearing to be well mannered get transformed into a brute mob instantaneously with opening of the doors of metro coaches. People try to elbow each other out and in, not caring even about older people, women and children. There is nothing unusual in this for anyone anymore.

Often people get hurt due to uncivilised behaviour of fellow metro travellers but the madness continues as if it is the last train from the station and those who would remain back would never make it!

Despite perpetual reminders on the public announcement system that those who are getting down from the Metro coaches should be allowed to deboard first and then people should start boarding the coach, hardly anyone follows this rule.

The situation is no different at any Metro station in Delhi and its suburbs, wherever metro has reached.

Pankaj had observed many people who get down from the Metro trains cursing and often abusing people who don't allow them to deboard easily with pushes and shoves to enter the coach without allowing other passengers to deboard.

Ironically when many of them get ready to catch another Metro they start behaving exactly like those whom they were cursing a few minutes ago.

They often used to discuss this kind of "uncivilised behaviour" in the newsroom and they had reached a common conclusion: "Travelling on a Metro in Delhi is a great learning experience if you want to study the human behaviour especially the darker aspects."

Whenever the Metro train stopped at stations where a few seats were vacant within coaches and a huge number of people rushed into the coaches, they train for seats in a way that reminded Pankaj of images of flood victims running for a loaf of bread after being hungry for a week. He had seen these images several times on television, he hadn't got the opportunity to cover such a tragedy so far.

Another darker aspect of the human nature stared him in face every time Pankaj travelled in Metro as men often pretended to be sleep or doze with their eyes closed as soon as an old man or a woman came and stood in front of them. The passengers who manage to get a seat just do not want to loose the comfort of a seat to a wanting old man, woman or small children. How selfish a man could be! How low one could stoop! This life of deception they live day in and day out just because they do not want to offer the seats! You lie to yourself just because you don't want to give your seat for 20 minutes to a person who needs it more than you! Do we live in a city full of two-legged animals? Don't we?

Though the good thing is that many times, some of the passengers intervene and force such able bodied utterly selfish creatures pretending to be human beings, to vacate their seats and make the old, the women and the children take these seats.

Pankaj had told one of the Public Relations Officer (PRO) of Delhi Metro Rail Corporation (DMCR) when he met him for the first time, "This is disgusting behaviour? Why don't you do something to tame these shameless passengers in metro. They flout every norm. They play loud music on mobiles, often misbehave with girls and women, squat near doors though you are not allowed to sit in metro on floor."

The PRO, who was a young officer, had put his hand on Pankaj's shoulder said, "Pankaj, there are far too many. We have invited citizens to come and join a special team that we are constituting so that they can enforce these rules. But no government authority can force people to behave in a civilized manner in matters of public transport."

Pankaj had been realizing lately this young officer was right. The problem with most of the Delhiites is that they lack civic sense. The worst part is that they are not even aware of it because this is the way they have seen their parents, uncles, aunts, cousins living happily!.

❑

8

Better Late Than Never

His mobile phone rang again. Pankaj was entering his office building. He was electrified. The same voice. The same sweet voice. The same voice that left him numb.

"Hello?"

"Hello, Hello…Hey Pankaj are you there?"

"Yes, This is Pankaj"

"Hey I am Sameera here..what happened to you. You picked up the phone and you were not saying anything..are you OK?"

Pankaj realized now that it was Sameera.

. "How can this happen, How I can misjudge her voice? I think it was her." He was telling himself.

Sameera snapped, "Pankaj, where are you? You are not sounding good. I am worried. Where are you?"

He came back into real world. "Oh! nothing Sameera, I am fine, I am just fine, don't worry."

"No, you are not fine... where are you?"

"I am just in front of our office building…where are you?"

"Come upstairs, I am in office.."

"OK …..I will be there in two minutes…"

He disconnected the mobile phone and as a matter of habit just checked whether his wallet was there in the back pocket of his jeans, his pen in front pocket and his note pad in his bag which he carried everyday to office. He shook his head. He was feeling a little giddy. He wanted to go back home and stand under a cold shower to make his head clear. It was just like a hangover whenever he used to cross his usual dose of three large pegs.

But he didn't drink last evening. Not even day before.

As soon as he reached near the lift, the phone rang again.

He picked up the phone. This time he was more careful.

Is it the same voice? It sounded like that. But he didn't want to take any chances.

"Pankaj here."

"Hi, Mr. Pankaj, this is Nisha...."

Pankaj got a bolt from the blue. He was so happy that he wanted to scream and at the same time there was a feeling of numbness. The lift door opened and closed. He just stood there listening to what his "dream girl" was saying.

"Mr. Pankaj, I am calling from the marketing department of 'YOUR GYM', the best gym in the town. Our gym has a corporate deal with your organization where we give staffers of your organization 50 per cent discount on annual membership of our gym..."

A pause.

A small pause of few seconds. Pankaj felt giddy again. Has the phone got disconnected...Again. Oh God! This cannot happen to me. Not now, not for a few more seconds till I take down her phone number or fix up a meeting with her or probably if nothing else could listen to her voice for a few more minutes, if not possible, "God give me atleast few more seconds before she goes off the line.."

The prayers were heard. The voice crackled on the phone again.

"Mr. Pankaj, are you there...?"

"Oh yes. I am here, I mean.. I am there, I mean...," Pankaj fumbled.

"I mean I am listening. Please go ahead."

"Thanks. So I was telling you that a number of employees of your esteemed organization have joined our gym and our feedback is that they are really happy that they took this decision."

There was a beep sound. It indicated "call waiting" to Pankaj. But he was in no mood to pick up another call and disconnect this one.

"I would like you to join our gym for a free trial period of 15 days. No charges. I would like to tell you about the facilities at our gym…"

Pankaj interjected sheepishly. "I know, I know about the benefits…errr facilities at your gym. My friends have told me. I think I won't mind coming for a trial period".

He wanted to shoot his next question, "When can I meet you?" But he curbed his instincts and told her very politely, "What would be an appropriate time to come and fill up the form?"

"How are you placed today? You can come anytime till evening. I am here."

"Great! I will come and see you after an hour."

"Thanks. I am looking forward to meet you."

Pankaj wanted to say, "Me too.."

The phone got disconnected. Pankaj looked at the screen to check the number and noticed "two missed" calls staring at him. Both were from Sameera. The phone rang again. It was Sameera, "Pankaj…," She was sounding panicky now.

"Hold, hold on, I am in the lift."

The lift door opened and he just pushed himself inside while disconnecting the phone. As soon as the lift stopped at his office floor he rushed towards the entry gate. He quickly punched his attendance card and the door got opened. The receptionist smiled. Pankaj sometimes thought. "What a difficult job! She has to keep on smiling. The most difficult thing to do these days!!"

He reached reporting room and found a worried Sameera standing there waiting for him. A few reporters were trying to look busy by staring at their computer screens and fiddling with keyboards. There were five of them. The rest hadn't come yet.

Sameera came to him. He knew by this time now that a typhoon is on the way. The only way to keep things under control was to take her to the office canteen.

"Hey! I missed my breakfast today. Let's go to cafetaria and eat something. I am dying of hunger," Pankaj tried to appear normal as he tried to build a protective shield to bear the forthcoming onslaught of a raging tempest which was standing in front of him.

The expressions on her face were a mix of anger, disgust, worry and helplessness. The tempest could blow anyway now!

Sameera's head was buzzing with lava of anger which she wanted to take out on him. She was so worried as Pankaj had sounded pretty abnormal on phone and then when she called him up his phone was busy and he did not pick up the phone. "What the hell is going on?," she wanted to scream and ask.

"This is weird," a part of her mind was trying to reason.

"He always picks up my call even when he is driving." It had never happened over the last two years that he didn't pick up her call. There were times when Sameera called him up at two in the night and told him she was disturbed and just wanted to talk to him. Mostly, she ended up crying but feeling much lighter deep inside after the conversation with him. Except a very few, now Pankaj was privy to most of the skeletons in her closet. She probably shared so much with him because he never asked any questions ever about her personal life. He was so unlike most of the guys these days who ask too many questions in the garb of caring. Probably they are genuine questions but she didn't like such probing. That is why her first dates never converted into the second ones. Except a relationship for three years she had in college, she had no relationship for almost four years now.

Sameera remembered vividly, "Vishesh was such a nice guy. A little weird. But he was fine otherwise. She liked him.

She was always with him all the time and everyone though that she was in love with him and he was in love with her. They went to discos, wild night outs, beer binges but all with friends. Never, never the two of them were alone in a way the lovers try to get a few moments when they can cuddle up.

She never proposed to him and he also never proposed her. But they were a happy go lucky couple. And then after final year when she joined mass communication course, they just drifted apart. A few months after that Vishesh called her up and proposed her on phonc but by that time she had realized, he was not the person with whom she wanted for to spend the rest of her life.

They were not in touch after that. It has been almost four years. A few of them proposed her during her PG-diploma course in mass communications from Indian Institute of Mass Communications, Delhi but she ever even cared to respond to them.

Pankaj held her hand and was almost dragging her to the cafeteria. A few raised eyebrows in the reporting room but they knew both of them get along very well. Initially some of the fellow colleagues tried to cook stories about the "blooming affair" between the two. But then they realized they just get along very well and are real good friends.

It is a bliss to have such colleagues who don't cook stories behind your back about your personal preferences.

Sameera didn't utter a single word. Pankaj was eating butter toast. She knew he was not hungry. But it was a ploy to buy some more time expecting the angry lava would subside down and he wouldn't have to face a volcano. Both of them deployed same tactics when anyone of them was angry.

"So what happened….?," Sameera broke the silence.

"Nothing…" Pankaj said while wiping butter from stained fingers with tissue paper.

"Hmmmmm……," Sameera said. Lava was boiling!

Pankaj knew the situation could get out of hand anytime now. He will have to do something and do something now.

"Look, I was just not feeling well..probably lack of sleep..I couldn't sleep properly last night. And then after I told you I am coming upstairs, a "source" called up. He had some interesting information. So I was talking to him on phone when you called up again. I couldn't disconnect that call and by the time I finished this conversation, I saw two missed calls from you. I am sorry but I am sure you understand. It was not intentional."

Sameera gave the parting shot after keeping Rs. 35 on the table (Rs. 20 for the butter toast and Rs. 10 for two cups of tea they had ordered. The rest was tip), "Look Pankaj, I think I know you quite well. I was worried as you sounded very weird. It's OK if you don't want to tell me the truth, I won't push you for that..."

She got up and waited for a shocked Pankaj to get up from his seat as this was not typical reaction from Sameera. Both of them started walking back towards the reporting room which was on the same floor. Pankaj knew, Sameera was hurt because of his erratic behaviour. He felt hurt too that he had done this to her.

"What am I supposed to do? What am I going to tell her? I am not sure myself. May be I can tell her that I think I am in love with a girl who had forgotten her mobile in Metro and I met her for four minutes at a crowded Metro Station to hand her back her phone."

This was already sounding absurd, Pankaj was telling himself. No one can believe that someone would fall in love like this. This is straight out from Bollywood. People would make fun of him, may be Sameera would burst out laughing too. He didn't want to explain this to anyone and he didn't want to feel embarrassed too and he was not sure whether even Sameera would be able to understand this "love at first sight" experienced by him.

Sameera looked at his face and she could see some conflict deep inside him shades of which were getting reflected on his face.

She took a deep breath and realized she has to let it go for the time being. She knew him too well. He would not tell her now but he would tell her surely, she knew.

❑

9

Dateline Dantewada

It was Wednesday. Pankaj had just reached office when he heard that 73 Central Reserve Police Force personnel have been massacred by the Maoists at Dantewada in Chattisgarh. A pall of gloom had descended over the newsroom though it was a big and exciting news story, what they call in journalism—"Story of the day". But more than a story, it was a tragedy.

Though he was a part of the city team but as the news snippets kept on flowing on newswires, the buzz was gaining momentum in the city reporting room.

"What the hell do you mean by that? What can they do, there women get raped by the local contractors and Patwaris. They do not have basic civic amenities, no education, no health care and no future. They have nothing to lose. For them there is still no freedom from the colonial rule. They continue to be exploited by the brown *sahibs* instead of *gora sahib*," Rashmi was arguing with Sameera trying to justify this attack by left extremists known as Maoists.

Rashmi was from Bihar. She had done her post-graduation in political science from Jawahar Lal Nehru University in Delhi, a hub of leftist ideology. She had become a member of one of the militant leftist student organization in JNU campus during her college days. There are several shades of left present there, from moderate left to extreme left. It is probably one of the last red bastions in India where the left has been able to maintain its stronghold atleast over the student community.

Her parents wanted her to take civil services examination. But she had decided to first go to academics. In between she fell in love with Dhananjay who was an year junior to him. Dhananjay was from Jharkhand.

She still remembered vividly that night. She was back home in Bihar when Dhananjay called her up on her cell phone.

"Listen carefully Rashmi, I am leaving for the jungle. I don't know when will I come back. If you won't be there when I come back, I won't mind that. I understand."

Rashmi knew what he was talking about. There was silence on both sides for few minutes. Rashmi only said three sentences, "Good Luck Dhananjay. I will wait for you. I am proud of you." Ever since then, everyday Rashmi opened the newspaper with a dreadful thought everyday that she might read somewhere, "Top Naxal ideologue Dhananjay killed in an encounter". Every morning when she found that the news item was not there, she had a sigh of relief.

Rashmi, at the core of her heart was all for the Maoist dictum—"Power flows from the barrel of gun". She had seen in her Own village how the dalits and the lower castes were exploited. She believed that to bring an end to this violence perpetrated on large sections of the society by a handful of power hungry pack of wolves there is no other way except a bloody revolution.

Dhananjay didn't call her back for months. She would discreetly get some messages from him through a messenger who would drop a letter at times in her one room rented accommodation at Mukherjee Nagar in North Delhi.

Earlier it was only ideological but now she had a personal stake in the Maoist movement. She would argue and argue and argue with anyone and everyone about the cause she supported. Though lately, she had withdrawn herself after someone cautioned her in the office, "It is not good to voice your views so openly in support of Maoists. You could be in trouble, after all the owner of the newspapers is a member of Rajya Sabha from the ruling party and the Prime Minister himself has said more than once that Maoism is the gravest threat to the country."

But today the atmosphere was different. Rashmi was alone unlike the past when she found many others in office often supporting her. Though several of them had not even visited a single village ever but being radical is being progressive! That is the easiest way to be progressive, so why not?

The arguments and counter-arguments on Maoist violence were reverberating in the reporting section.

Then suddenly Pankaj was reminded, he had to go to the gym at the ground floor to meet what could be "love of his life." Pankaj was embarrassed at these thoughts.

Is it influence of Paul Coelho whose novels he had been reading these days. He had just finished "The Alchemist" and was starting of on "Zaheer".

"I need to do something about this, I can't think like this. This just doesn't make sense. I have seen her a few times and properly met her once and it is by sheer chance that she called me up again as an employee of the gym which is in the same building where I work. And I am going berserk. Am I?"

He shook his head, checked his watch, looked at the gory visuals of some of the slain CRPF personnel flashed on the screen of the TV which was tucked away in one corner of the reporting section. It generally remained mute and reporters just used it for checking the scroll at the bottom of the screen where news channels flash the latest news. Who wants to listen to the TV anchors gloating all over themselves most of time? Ironically, more than the news they are interested in telling the viewers that they are the first one to broadcast it.

Alok standing next to Pankaj, remarked in his characteristic style, "Idiots! They are really idiots! Every channel is saying these are exclusive visuals and they are all showing the same visuals." None of the national news channels had actually got the visuals themselves. They were broadcasting the visuals being shown by a local TV channel of Chattisgarh, the logo of the local channel was visible on the right hand side corner of the visuals being played by all the channels.

With frenzy of the TV newsroom getting reflected in the loud and overexcited voice and mannerisms of TV anchors, the innocent viewers were being taken for ride once again as correspondents sitting in Raipur, the State capital of Chattisgarh, which is 345 kms away from Dantewada and almost 400 km away from the spot where this incident happened, kept on doling out pearls of wisdom as if they witnessed this whole thing with their own eyes.

Pankaj took a deep breath. Surprisingly he didn't find himself moved by this tragedy at Chattisgarh. Earlier there were days when he would remain disturbed over any such massacres. How men kill men, how people exploit people, how nature kills men and women and children, how the so-called civilized societies plunder natural wealth and exploit the weaker ones – Pankaj was getting closer and closer to the ground realties with every passing day in journalism and more than often he felt offended by the way things went around him.

But today, it was different. He had to meet someone. He was a little surprised that there were not even pangs of guilt consciousness in him that he is not agitated over killing of 73 security personnel by Maoists in one of the most daring ambushes in the history of Maoist movement in this country so far.

Pankaj checked his watch, it was 4 p.m. He looked around. Thank God! Sameera was not there. She had left after heated arguments with Rashmi to cover a press conference. Alok was busy watching TV and in between barking orders to a bunch of reporters to take reactions of pro-Maoist and anti-Maoist intellectuals in the city over this incident. One of the reporters was asked to talk to some retired officials of the CRPF and Intelligence Bureau. Fortunately Pankaj was spared.

Pankaj went to the washroom, washed his face and suddenly realised that his hair were too short and he looked a little funny. He also realized that unlike most his friends he never kept a pocket comb. That made him feel a little depressed "Why would she fall for me? I am not that handsome. There are many more good looking people than me."

But still he wanted to meet her. "Let's see, what happens," he thought.

❑

10

Just Friends?!

His hand touched hers. She was trying to maintain a distance. But there were too many people in the Metro coach.

"So I was telling you….," Before Pankaj could complete what he wanted to say, he suddenly felt being pushed. People standing a few feet apart were trying to accommodate a group of tourists who had just entered the coach from Akshardham Metro Station.

Before he could complete his sentence, Pankaj realized that his back was pressed against the doors of the metro which remained closed as people were entering from the doors on the opposite side.

Then a big push from the fellow-travellers and Sameera had to hold Pankaj first from the shoulder and then at his waist to hold her balance. People were still trying to enter the coach even as the security guard was trying to stop them from doing so.

Pankaj suddenly felt the warmth of Sameera's breath. There was a familiar odour too which he liked. Her body was now almost overlapping him with not even a millimetre of space to move around. Pankaj's face was flushed red so was Sameera's. By default, it was the first time they came so close physically. Sensuality grows up on physical proximity. It was available in plenty to both Pankaj and Sameera, at this moment.

She was as much aroused as Pankaj was. Their bodies were hard pressed against each other. It was awkward, embarrassing but both of them were not in a position to utter a single word. While Pankaj tried to stare at some vague point on the ceiling of the metro coach, Sameera was searching for any such point on the floor so that she could fix her gaze there, till they get a little more room to stand apart. And Pankaj could feel every inch of Sameera's body. Sameera could feel the mixed fragrance of Park Avenue aftershave lotion and Park Avenue deodorant which Pankaj religiously stuck to.

Surprisingly for Sameera, after a few minutes she was not uncomfortable with it. The metro had crossed Yamuna Bank Station and the situation in coach had remained almost same. The number of travellers who left the coach at Yamuna Bank equalled almost the number of passengers who boarded Metro from there.

Pankaj, though, was a little bit uncomfortable with it. He tried to think about Nisha but it seemed Sameera's body had taken control over his mind. This realisation made him even more uncomfortable.

He was on fire. Sameera sheepishly looked at him. She was on fire too. They stood still waiting for this mayhem to be over. It took them another 10 minutes before the train reached at Mandi House Metro Station where they got a little breather.

Both of them were now able to stand at a little distance from each other.

Sameera was not her usual self till they reached Rajiv Chowk Metro Station where she got down to take another Metro to go to her place.

Pankaj was still dazed and could hardly reply with a feeble "bye" in reply to Sameera's bye and waving hands.

"What the hell is happening to me? She is a friend. I never thought about her this way," Pankaj was arguing with himself.

Sameera was sitting dazed in the first coach of the Metro which is permanently reserved for ladies. She could still feel that she was aroused. She never wanted to get out of that metro. She just wanted to hold him, hug him, kiss him and wanted him to make love to her.

After a long time she felt emotionally secure and physically alive during those few minutes from Akshardham to Mandi House. She realized that she just do not remember that what had actually happened during those 13 minutes around her.

She was completely mesmerized. Her body was on fire. And she just wanted him to be with her in bed.

The train suddenly came to halt with a jolt and she fortunately heard the announcement at the nick of time. This is "Vishwavidyalya" Metro Station. "The doors will open on the.."

She didn't had to listen further as she knew where the doors will open and like a pre-programmed robot she got up from her seat, picked her bag and zipped pass several commuters getting out of the coach.

It was hell of a night for both of them. Had there been two cameras panned in their bedrooms and the footage of both could be shown simultaneously on a screen split into two, it would have made an amazing reality TV show.

Both of them were tossing in the bed. They wanted to sleep but couldn't. Their mind rushed back to the same old 13 minutes when they were so close that they had never been so close to anyone like this for a long time.

They were realizing, for the first time, that between them apart from the bond of friendship, perhaps something else also existed. Was it love, longing, infatuation or lust? They were trying to figure out.

Sameera tried to flip through the pages of some magazines but couldn't. She had the urge to pick up her mobile and tell Pankaj that she has realized that she wanted him and she wanted him badly.

Pankaj, on the one other hand, was dreading that she shouldn't call up but somewhere deep in his mind he knew that he wouldn't mind an opportunity to sleep with her. He respected their friendship but these were his "weak moments" if one may call them weak.

"This will complicate issues," he was trying to make himself understand. Or probably it already had complicated issues, his mind was on a whirlwind tour picking up all kind of assumptions and making bizarre presumptions.

He was 25 and still hadn't slept with a woman. Sameera was 24 and still virgin. They had never thought about these things earlier so forcefully. Most of their friends had lost their virginity and were quite contented to do so.

What scared Pankaj was that he was enduring those moments of physical proximity with none else but Sameera.

Sameera didn't know what to do too. She got up from her bed and went to the bathroom. Standing in front of the bathroom mirror, she dropped her clothes and looked at herself with eye of a beauty peagent judge. She pouted her full luscious lips and she tried to judge how attractive she was. She untied her shoulder length hair and then a smile, a wicked smile, appeared on her face. She whispered to herself, "Oh Pankaj! I love you and I want you."

Pankaj got up from his bed and picked up the water bottle placed at a stool near his bed. He took big swigs till the bottle was empty and when he kept it down he realized that even though the air conditioner was on, there were drops of sweat on his forehead. He went to the bathroom and washed his face.

After coming back, he just pushed the curtains open and peeped at the tranquillity that had enveloped the ever busy colony road. He looked at the half moon which appeared to be moving among the dark clouds and realized it has been ages since he looked at the moon.

He looked at the clock on the wall whose dial was glistening and making a loud announcement without a noise that it was 3.30 a.m.

Sameera was dreaming now. She was in Pankaj's arms. He was kissing her. She held him tightly. Their lips met and they pounced upon each other like two hungry bears.

There was a loud sound. The dream stood shattered by the alarm tone of her mobile phone. It was 7 a.m. She opened her eyes and basked in the glory of those heavenly moments in her dreams and then a pall of gloom descended on her as she realized that Pankaj is on where near her.

She shook her head, got up and sat in bed for another 45 minutes before the door bell rang. She really had to make an effort to go to the door and unlatch it. Standing in front of her was a small kid of eight years.

"My mother will not come today," he told her. Sameera smiled at him and said OK. The message simply meant that she will have to clean the house herself and wash the dishes too as her maid Rani was not coming today.

Pankaj was woken up by the beep sound on his mobile phone. He opened his tired eyes with an effort and tried to grab the phone lying on his computer table by his bed side. He stretched his hand but couldn't reach it.

The beep sound just refused to go away. So he had to get up. He picked up the mobile phone and with a yawn looked at the screen of the phone. "Message from Nisha" it read. "Hi, Can we talk?" The timing of the message was 9.59 a.m.

Pankaj suddenly felt giddy. He had an inkling about what she was going to talk probably. Or may be he was just assuming it.

"The first thing I need is a cold water bath to clear my head," he told himself and moved towards the bathroom attached to his room.

But while moving towards the bathroom he sent back a text message to her saying, "Call u bk."

"It took him 35 minutes to get ready. He couldn't eat much. His mother seemed worried." You didn't eat anything last night and now you are just having a toast and a cup of tea in breakfast? "Are you OK?"

On any other day Pankaj would have smiled back and told his mother not to worry. But today he didn't reply. He, in fact, was thinking about what Nisha would like to talk about. She had never sent a message like that ever since they had met. He knew that she knew by this time that he liked her and he also had an inkling that she liked him too. But how much? That was the big question.

He, like most of the men, was not able to gauge the feelings of a particular woman towards himself.

Pankaj's mother asked twice and then when she held his arm and shook him a little bit, he realized that his mother was asking him about his well being. "Oh don't worry Mom, I am fine, I am just fine. It is just that my stomach is a little upset so I do not want to eat much."

"Then why don't you take a medicine?"

"I will Mom, I will buy something on my way to office."

Pankaj was in a hurry to talk to Nisha now. He realized that it has been almost one hour since she had sent a message to him.

"Why don't you take the car today,?" His father said and Pankaj realized that he had not noticed that he too had been sitting there.

"No Dad, I am fine. I can take a metro. You may need the car at home."

"I don't need it and your mother also doesn't have to go anywhere today, so you can take it."

"Pankaj thought for a minute while sipping tea. He wanted some peace and a few moments alone. In Metro there is too much of noise and there are too many people around."

"Ok Dad, I will take the car."

He put his cup down, went to his room to pick up his bag. He went to the keystand where keys of his father's Wagon R were hanging and took the keys.

After driving about a km he stopped his car in a service lane which cuts the T point leading to Ring Road near Raja

Garden and dialled Nisha's number. All that his bouncing heart which was almost ready to pop out got was sound of "engaged" and a pre-recorded message from the mobile service operator, "The person you are trying to call is busy on another line. To leave a voice message…..". Pankaj disconnected the phone and made another call. He tried thrice and couldn't get her. Her phone was constantly busy.

"She can't be talking to her father or brother for so long. She can't be talking to a client for so long and moreover she never called up any client from her mobile phone. Then who is she talking to?"

The question added to the irritation level.

"I will make one last try," Pankaj thought and put his finger on the mobile phone's redial button but before he could push it, the screen started blinking "Incoming Call." The screen was also showing caller's name –Sameera.

❑

11

Yes it is! No, it is not!

As the metro chucked past the Rajinder Nagar Metro Station, Pankaj could see a man was lying on the floor of the station. A woman was sitting beside her. She was trying to revive him and the man looked unconscious. The figures were blurred as the train was moving and Pankaj could not make much.

He was surprised to see that no one was there to help her. It seemed that the man must have been lying there for at least a few minutes. "No wonder, this is Delhi. *Dilliwalas* don't care for anyone except for themselves."

The train had crossed two more stations. It was 11.30 a.m. Pankaj was lost in his thoughts. His mobile crackled. Pankaj pushed the green button and without realizing, just as a matter of habit, spoke, "Pankaj here".

He was brought back to reality. "Hi Pankaj, this is Nisha. Are you OK?"

"Why? What happened to me? I am fine," Pankaj said.

"Ok! I was a little worried that you haven't been coming to the gym for the last three days."

Silence.

More Silence.

Pankaj was thinking what should he say.

He would analyse it a little later that what it meant when a girl he hardly know for three weeks has started showing concern for him.

He would argue with himself, “Why is she worried?”

Then he would answer it himself. “Probably she likes me too.”

Then his own glee was killed by his journalistic tendency to be doubtful about every good thing that happens around. “Oh, don’t be an emotional fool. She is a sharp professional, she just wants to ensure that clients brought by her should continue to come to the gym.”

“Hello! Hello! Pankaj, are you there?” Before Pankaj could reply there was that dismal long beep sound with a message on the mobile screen, “Call failed”.

It simply meant that his mobile’s connectivity with the mobile operator’s network had got disrupted. Pankaj looked around and realized the reason for that. The train had entered the underground tunnel which connected R. K. Ashram Marg Station to the Rajiv Chowk Metro Station.

It was weird he thought as some people continued to talk on mobile phone around him while some others were saying, “Hello! Hello! Hello….” without realizing that they are making too much of noise.

He took a deep breath, shook his head, picked his bag and stood behind around a dozen people getting ready to jostle with the unruly crowd that would try to enter the coach at Rajiv Chowk Metro Station. They just won’t allow the passengers here to come out.

There was sweat and abundance of body odour around him mixed up with varied aromas of perfumes and deodorants used by some of the more suave people who took care that their body odour do not hurt passengers around them. But most of the passengers don’t use it.

At the cost of being appearing a snob, Pankaj had often raised this issue with his colleagues over drinks though in a much lighter vein. Whenever there was a huge traffic jam on main roads in Delhi, which was more then often now, his hurried colleagues who suffered such jams would tell him that they were really jealous of him that he could catch a metro to work and back home everyday avoiding such draconian traffic snarls.

Pankaj would often respond by saying, "But I have to suffer a greater ordeal than you, when people after eating onions and garlic in the breakfast or lunch, stand there burping. Add to this the sickening body odour they have. If you are standing next to them, you really have to make an effort not to faint."

"Snobs are snobs and they will always be snobs! And I am proud of being a snob if that means living a healthy and peaceful life!"

That was Sameera's one liner to end such discussions.

Meanwhile Pankaj was back on his train of thoughts as he got down at the Rajiv Chowk Metro Station and started his routine stroll towards the office.

It was drizzling outside. It is supposed to rain in first week of July in Delhi.

But the joke is that if the Met Department says, it will rain, you can comfortably put your umbrellas back in the cupboards as it is never going to rain.

Alas! The joke is much closer to the reality than the Met predictions are. "Blame it on the very nature of that branch of science which deals with weather predictions. Even God cannot predict it right, if you ask me," a senior Met Department Official had confided to him in an irritated tone sometime ago. He eventually became a good friend and graduated further to become a good "Source" for Pankaj. Though the information he used to offer failed to find space in news pages more than often.

His mobile reminded him of its existence again with a sound of "ping". He read the message, "Will u b coming 2 gym today?- Nisha".

He felt good. She was missing him, it seems. He reprimanded himself again, "Don't read too much. Don't be a journalist when it comes to personal messages. Don't read between the lines."

He decided to finish his work early and go to the gym.

Nisha was a little surprised with herself. It has been a few weeks only that she had met Pankaj. "What a decent guy he is!" She had told Lata with an exclamation mark written all over her face.

Lata had responded with a smile, "You are gone!"

"What do you mean *yaar*? I am just saying that he is a decent guy, he doesn't stare at girls from head to toe, the way most of the guys do in this city."

"Why only guys, the older men are even greater devils. Age, caste, religion is no bar. They are all like that," Lata added fuel to the fiery discussion they were having.

Nisha was really impressed by Pankaj's attitude towards her. There were other reasons too. After she joined "YOUR Gym" as Assistant Marketing Manager, he was the first client she was able to tap. He never asked for her cell number. He never tried to find whether she lived alone. He never wore the glamour of being a journalist up his sleeve.

He was different. He didn't prefer to listen to new Bollywood songs. He was a film buff. He was very well read and humble and could talk about anything under the sun. And he dressed very simply, no flashy colours.

She felt comfortable and at times secure when he was around.

For the last few days they had started travelling back from office to home together. Most of the time his colleague Sameera was also with them. They jelled together well but she realized at times that Sameera was possessive about him.

So there was an undercurrent of a little strain between the two girls which Pankaj, probably, had not realized or felt.

They talked about all sort of things—movies, office politics, books, comics, songs, friends and most of all dreams as they trudged along from their office building to the Rajiv Chowk Metro Station.

And then he almost vanished around a week ago. He was not coming to gym where Nisha generally could come and meet him while he was doing some workout.

She also used to meet Sameera at times. It was good when Pankaj was alone and not with Sameera. She could stand and talk to him for a few minutes.

There were some other office colleagues of Pankaj too who used to come there but Nisha avoided them. As best as she could.

The work was fine, the organization was not paying her well but it was just fine for a start up job for a fresher.

She had decided to call up Pankaj and ask why he was not coming to the gym but then she realized that it would not be right thing to do. In fact, she wanted to ask Lata, "Should I call him? He hasn't come to the gym for a couple of days atleast, he has not messaged me for the last two days and I am travelling home back alone on the metro."

In a few weeks time she had got so used to the new routine. At around 8.30 p.m. Pankaj messaged her that he would be moving out in ten minutes and he is wrapping up his day's work. Nisha, whose work generally got finished by 7.30 p.m. tried to keep herself busy with some useless office work or would keep reading the names of the clients she was supposed to call up over the next few days.

In fact she had read this list so many times that now she remembered almost every one's name along with their mobile numbers.

Between 8.45 p.m. to 9 p.m. Pankaj will come down and find Nisha standing outside the gym's door. If Sameera also finished the work then both Pankaj and Sameera would come down together. And it was always same, Pankaj with a slight tilt of his head listening and Sameera with excitement written all over her face would be talking in hush-hush tone.

The three or two of them, if Sameera is not there, would start their 15 minutes walk towards Rajiv Chowk Metro Station. After reaching inside the station, Sameera would take stairs and trot down to catch the metro going towards

"Vishwavidyalaya" while Pankaj and Nisha would cross over a small foot overbridge and reach the platform to board Metro going towards Dwarka.

At times they talked, at times they didn't. She felt good just being with him. She never had this feeling. She liked it, relished it and longed for it though she refused to accept it.

Sunday evenings were no more fun for her. She would wait for Monday to arrive so that she could walk back with him to the Metro station.

And then for one week, Pankaj had vanished. In fact, he had rushed to Uttarakhand where there were flash floods and he was sent on an emergency assignment. He had left very late in the night after he got a call from his Chief Reporter.

He had just reached his home. It was around 10 p.m., when Alok called him up and told him, "There are flash floods in Uttarakhand, We are sending you there. A photographer will be going with you. The office car will reach you by midnight, the driver will give you a packet. It has Rs. 10,000 as advance money for the tour. Take your laptop and data card with you. You will reach Dehradun by ten in morning. From there, find out which are the most severely affected areas. Take the office car or hire a vehicle, we have alerted our Dehradun correspondent that you would be coming, he will make all the arrangements."

It took a week for Pankaj to go there and come back. From Dehradun, he went to Uttarkashi. What they called "office car" was actually a Toyota Innova, which was a sturdy and comfortable vehicle to travel in mountains. The driver, an employee of the organization, was experienced and a jovial guy. He himself was from Garhwal area of Uttarakhand so the travelling was made easier.

From Dehradun, Pankaj went to Chamoli district. On the way to Dehradun from Delhi, the photographer Sukesh had bought three bottles of whiskey and one bottle of Rum. Pankaj had aksed him, "Why so many bottles?"

"*Zarrorat padegi* (we will need this)," Sukesh replied with a smile on his face. "This is your first assignment, I believe, to cover a natural calamity in mountains."

Sukesh who was atleast 10 years senior to Pankaj in profession was a "hell of a guy" as Pankaj described him later. A thorough professional, a heavy drinker but very helpful. He was an expert in covering such tough assignments.

He told Pankaj with a smile, "I hate to say this but you are going to enjoy this assignment buddy and this is where you can do real stories. Attending press conferences in five star hotels in Delhi is not journalism. So it is your moment, grab it and do as many good stories as you can."

So Pankaj grabbed it. His first stop was Chamoli district where flash floods and cloud bursting had washed a school away. Ten children had died.

When he reached the spot, there were only debris. The roads had also been washed away. They had left their vehicle where the last shred of what you may call a road remained and walked for six hours to reach the spot.

It was going to be dark soon. They had reached their at around 2 p.m., two days after they had left Delhi. So far Pankaj had filed a couple of routine stories while travelling on way to Chamoli where the real devastation had happened. Sukesh was clicking his camera like a machine. He was using a camera with film rolls as well as digital cameras.

❑

12

Dateline Chamoli

In the backdrop of picturesque Himalayas, Pankaj was trying to absorb the shock of debris strewn all around him. In the middle of this heap of rubble which, before destruction, was a school, Pankaj was standing. He was taken aback. He was forcing himself to imagine what would have been the scene inside the school when boulders, water and a slush of mud had hit the school building. The school was up to class V. Around 120 students studied there. It was a government aided school. A broken board was lying on one side with name of the school Bal Vidya Mandir written on it.

While Sukesh was frantically clicking the pictures trying to get them from as many angles as he could, Pankaj was trying to reason with himself why Mother Nature should do this to small kids. Ten of them had died and three bodies were recovered. Eighty were rescued with minor injuries and there was still no trace of 10 others. They were lying somewhere under the debris.

There were a few other photographers and reporters also. They had come from, local editions of Hindi newspapers from Dehradun. There were no mikes, no camera crews from national channels there though some of the local videographers were filming it. They were, what you call in journalistic parleys, stringers. You may call them freelancers also. They would send their footage to the national TV channels through their laptops and would get a couple of thousand of rupees if their footage will be used on the national TV channels.

About 50 rescue workers from various government departments were trying to remove the debris. There were no modern equipment here which could expedite the removal of debris. "It is difficult to bring them on this terrain, more so, after the roads connecting this place have been washed away," a Block Development Officers told Pankaj who furiously scribbled this quote in his notebook.

"This is a good quote," Pankaj thought. It would establish the fact that the rescue work is not up to the mark, for whatever reasons. Anyway who cares to go into the reasons. What people want to know is that how the rescue work was going on. But do people in metros really want to know this? May be, may be not. May be it depends on the way this story is told.

"You have to make it glamourous and sexy, doesn't matter what the story is about," Pankaj was told once by a senior journalist in Press Club. The more gory details you have, the greater is the possibility to spice it up with what they call in newsrooms "a human angle". Then it is surely a blockbuster story. Pankaj had felt like puking after listening this. "How could you trivialise human tragedy like this?," he had argued.

"This is not trivialising. This our job. If you will file a simple story, why would someone want to read it. So search for spicy details—a family who lost it all, a woman who is pregnant and got widowed, children becoming orphans."

Pankaj had kept on looking at the face of this senior journalist who had moved from newspaper to television a few years ago and was considered to be one of the best reporters when it came to covering natural calamities or any other big human tragedy.

He didn't know how much truth was in it at that time. Many of his friends had cautioned him that journalism at times dehumanizes the journalists.

A part of Pankaj's mind was replaying all these moments of past as a grey shaded film while the other part of his mind was actively focusing on the "spot". He took out his mineral water bottle, took a swig and was about to light a cigarette for himself when he heard a shriek. A few metres away from him, he saw a woman collapsing. In front of her were two bodies. In almost split second everyone on the spot—rescue workers, villagers, families trying to locate their children, journalists, photojournalists, video journalists—all of them rushed towards the woman.

What Pankaj found about that woman translated into a story which was published next day on the page one of his newspaper with a screaming headline

"She lost it all……"
By Pankaj Malhotra
Chamoli, September 25

She lost it all. Rukmini Devi, 25, lost both her children—Six year old Varun and four year old Swaati to the massive cloudburst which struck off life of 10 children at Bal Vidya Mandir at Chamoli District. Worst, she had lost her husband two years ago and since then her in-laws had forced her to leave the house and live with her octogenarian mother.

"Rukmini witnessed the gory scene of bodies of her two children being taken out of debris……"

It was a blockbuster story.

❑

13

Games People Play With You

Boom! Boom!

Had they got guns they would have killed each other. And that too without an iota of remorse.

Nandini and Alok could be visualised at this moment by all and sundry in the office with the invisible guns in their hand and firing at each other brutally. It was not an online version of a new computer war game but it in fact reflected everyday realties of millions who toil hard in their workplaces spending more and more time to ward off the attacks by colleagues in a war game quite popular for those who win it and unpopular among those who lose it. It is called "Office politics."

Pankaj was entering the Reporters' Section with all kind of bizarre thoughts. He did not know how he would face Sameera today. There was something different ever since that ride in metro last evening.

"Did she feel the same way?"

He couldn't dare to think about an answer. Yet this question kept on popping in his mind.

"She seemed quite comfortable during that ride. May be I am thinking too much. But what do I do, every time I think about those moments what embarrasses me most is that I seemed to have enjoyed her body being pressed to mine."

He kept on struggling with the string of thoughts, wild imaginations and feelings which defied any logic.

Moreover he had not slept during night. His eyes were red and he was feeling tired not sleepy though. It is a miserable state. It happens often when we are tired but our minds are so active and trying to control some wild thoughts while the thoughts continue to defy all attempts to leash them.

The more one tries to control them, curb them, annihilate them, greater is the force with which they hit back.

You feel at sea with yourself. You can't help it. Probably a self-help book written on this issue would be the bestseller.

But Pankaj soon realized while sipping tea from a plastic cup after throwing himself in his chair that there is something going on.

He turned around to see and found that all his colleagues were trying to look busy staring at their computers while stealing glances towards the Chief Reporter's cubicle which had a glass door.

It was a small cubicle, nicely done up and was on one end of the reporting room.

He could hear the loud voices from Alok's chamber. There he saw the News Editor Nandini standing. Her chamber was next to Alok's cubicle.

They were never best of the friends. How could they be? In the business of news, the Desk and the Reporting departments are always at war. The desk people have the job to edit stories sent by reporters and place them on pages and produce the newspaper. The "deskies", as they are often called do a less glamorous job. They don't go out in the field. They have to be merciless in chopping, cutting, rewriting copies of reporters.

Throughout the world the animosity between the two departments is universal. The deskies feel that reporters file trash and the reporters feel that deskies sit in air conditioned offices and they have no idea what happens in the field from where they bring back reports after shedding "blood, sweat and tears."

The general perception about newspapers is that the journalists begin their day after mid-day. But the fact is that it starts very early. The reporters see their newspaper early morning and the first thing they do is to call the Chief Reporter and complain about how vital details about their stories have been eliminated mindlessly by some 'joker' on the desk. How the "headline" put up by the desk turns a brilliant story into a pedestrian piece of writing.

And the Chief Reporter looses no time to call up the editor. As News Editors, who head the desk, reach home after the newspaper goes to print, which is generally after one in the morning, so they get up late and are not disturbed by the editors before 11 in the morning unless some major goof-up is visible in the morning edition of the newspapers.

But before going back home, most of the battle-worn News Editors make it a point to send a long note in e-mail to the Editor about trash stories filed by reporters, how they did not file stories before the deadline and how they wrote patchy copies for the day. Any other issue they can get hold of about reporters is always a welcome addition to their long list of woes which they share with the Editor religiously day after day.

So as a newspaper Editor gets up in morning, the first mail she or he sees on blackberry phone is often a long list of complaints from the News Editor. By 8.30 a.m., the Chief Reporter calls up with a long list of his or her own complaints.

So by 9 a.m. everyday the battlefield is ready.

Pankaj thought that this must have got something to do with some important story not treated well or probably something which was not filed in time because of which the newspaper must have gone to printing press late.

Then he heard Nandini's voice, almost choking herself, "No way, I am not going to allow this to be put on my head!"

Alok retorted, "So what do you want, this should be put on my head? You are the one who wanted it, I never asked for it."

Nandini was a lady on the wrong side of forties. Generally pleasant, she was helpful. But she also had a stubborn attitude about certain things. She protected her clan of deskies like a fierce and injured lioness all the time and took less than few seconds to dash off stinkers in e-mail to reporters letting them know in an extremely official language what she thought of their work.

Pankaj had received one such e-mail from her last month which he still remembered. It read:

"Dear Pankaj,

"Your story on demolitions in the East Delhi was received well in time but all other newspapers have many more vital details which our story doesn't have. I am sure you would be careful about this in the future.

Cheers!

Nandini"

Pankaj had read this mail and stared at it even for a few minutes longer as a copy of mail was marked to his chief reporter as well as his Editor M.K. Mamgai.

"I don't know what is the problem with this woman. I had the best story. She still has to pick on me," he had told Sameera in frustration.

Sameera chuckled, "Oh ! come on Pankaj! I knew this had to happen."

Pankaj was confused, "How did you know? Why didn't you tell me if you knew?"

Sameera smiled sheepishly, "*Yaar* you are a *dhakkan*. Why don't you understand?"

Pankaj was even more frustrated by now, "Understand? What is there to understand?"

Sameera said nonchalantly, "Oh come on! the whole office knows that she has a crush on you. And you don't even look at her? What else would she do?"

Pankaj was first stunned and then started giggling, "Sameera, You are nuts. She is married. She has a teenaged son. You just can't think of anything else but.."

"Nahin, Sach mein yaar. Sahi keh rahi hoon. Everyone in the desk also knows she has a crush on you."

Pankaj had ended the conversation with, "Shut-up Sameera" and had left office in a huff to cover an assignment.

He was brought back from his flashback by the sound of "Bang". Nandini had banged the door of Alok's cubicle while coming out.

Six reporters looked up from their computer screens simultaneously at the slammed door. And with a sudden jerk, the door opened again after exactly 30 seconds.

Alok, huffing and puffing, shaking a little bit and looking even more shaken came almost running out and followed in the direction where Nandini had gone.

There was a hushed silence in the reporting room.

Everyone was dying to know what is this all about. And then the most informed person in the office, a treasure trove of office gossip entered the office.

Ramji Lal, the senior most peon in this office was coming with a tray of coffee cups for all six reporters.

As he placed the cup at Pankaj's table, Pankaj asked him two quick questions, "*Coffee ka order kisne diya* (who placed the order for coffee)?"

Quick came reply, "Sameera Madam ne. *Sabke liye mangwai hai* (Sameera Madam has ordered coffee for all)".

Pankaj took a deep breath. "Oh! That means everything is normal."

Whenever Sameera was in a jovial mood, she would order coffee for all the reporters in the section. That was known to everyone.

"That means she has not felt bad about yesterday. Pankaj felt as light as a feather."

Then came the second question, *"Kya maamla hai. Kis baat par jung chal rahi hai*? (What is the matter? What is the issue that has resulted in this war?)"

Ramji Lal always dressed impeccably in a light blue safari suit with black shining shoes. He was in early fifties and at one time used to be a firebrand leader of the Employees Union comprising the non-editorial staff.

But time changes. Most of the Union leaders were chucked out. Employees were made to shift to the contract system in late 1990s. That was the principle followed by most of the major news organizations in India.

Those who agreed to shift to the "contractual system" were spared and those who did not were pushed out of the organization on one pretext or the other. So by the year 2000, there was not even a single employee in "*The Daily*" which was left on contract.

Journalists were the first one to shift to contract system. There was some initial resistance which was broken by the management by transferring those not accepting their terms and conditions to the North-Eastern States.

These "cases" were an eye-opener for the rest. So all those who claimed to have the power of the pen which could move governments, were not able to move their management even by an inch.

Quietly, one after another they started accepting contracts which were renewable after every three years.

Now it was an accepted norm. No one even talked about it partly due to the fact that a whole generation of journalists and other non-journalist employees had accepted from being "permanent employees" to "employees on three-year-contract" had retired. There were many whose contracts were not renewed. Some got jobs in other newspapers, most didn't. No one knew what happened to them after sometime. Probably, no one even wanted to know, that would have made them feel even more helpless.

And people think journalists are the most powerful entities in this country!

Ramji Lal was the only one who used to narrate stories about the glorious past of this newspaper which had seen some of the best editors and doyens of this profession working here.

The idiosyncrasies of the old guard of this profession looked and sounded even more interesting when Ramji shared them with young journalists.

The unanimous opinion in reporting room was that Ramji was the best story-teller anyone of them had ever seen or heard.

Ramji was candid and very crafty when it came to revealing vital pieces of information.

He had worked and survived in this office for three decades where many big guns fell silent before their time had come and this long stint was made possible by one basic principle he had adopted. He would never reveal complete information about any office activity about which he is not supposed to know. He would break the information he has into interesting bits and pieces and along with tea and coffee he would keep on serving these tempting information capsules to editorial staff in office.

When these bits and pieces were put together, people could see the whole picture very clearly but no one could discredit Ramji that he was the one who had revealed this information.

Akanksha, a senior reporter in the reporting section had started calling Ramji "Wikileaks" of "*The Daily*". And the name was getting quite popular. Though Ramji didn't had any idea what it meant. His impeccable safaris and sheepish smile remained as it is.

By the time he had served coffee to all six reporters in the reporting section, he had once again demonstrated the exemplary skills of story telling by throwing interesting nuggets of vital information about Alok-Nandini spat.

Now all these pieces had to be just put together. And the six reporters did put it together by the time they had finished their coffee.

What emerged was so bizarre and yet so funny that all six were laughing at the end of it.

"I tell you this woman is nuts," Akanksha remarked.

"Hey don't say this about Nandini, Pankaj will feel bad," Sameera chuckled.

Pankaj, who has almost dozing off by now suddenly opened his eyes and realized what was being said about him and Nandini, another young reporter Rahul added, "You are right Sameera, Pankaj's stories always get special treatment from Nandini."

Pankaj tried to stop them, "Shut up, *yaar*, this is no time to make fun of me or anyone. This is something serious. I have never seen such a bitter fight between these two."

"But this is funny. How can two senior people fight over such a trivial issue?," Sameera said.

The story put together by these six reporters on the basis of, information provided by Ramji was like this:

"Three weeks ago Nandini wanted to get an exhaust fan installed in the Editing Section as some of her colleagues had complained that there was not enough fresh air and they felt suffocated especially during late evening hours.

Now Nandini wanted to get that exhaust fan installed on one of the walls of Alok's cubicle. The problem was that both the Desk and the Reporting section shared a common newsroom and Alok's and Nandini's chambers were the one which divided the two sections.

Alok outrightly refused that as he knew that the noise made by the exhaust fan would disturb him. Nandini didn't want to let this opportunity go away to show Alok and his Reporting team that in this organization the Desk will have the final say.

Alok was sharp and seasoned enough to guess the agenda behind this obscure looking move by Nandini. On the chessboard which we call office, this turned out to be another battle royale.

Now the question was who would have the final say? If Nandini was successful in getting an exhaust fan installed in Alok's chamber that would mean that Nandini is the real boss. If Alok is able to get the exhaust fan installed either in Nandini's chamber or in the area where deskies worked, then Alok would be seen as the real boss and that would clearly mean that the reporters could take their sweet revenge from the deskies.

It might sound bizarre to many who see it from outside but the fact remains that smaller issues riding on waves of big egos often create complexities. And as they say, that in the field of journalism, especially Indian journalism, there are too many 'small' people with too many of big egos.

Like a flashback, events spread over the last couple of years involving ego clashes amongst his colleagues started coming back to him. So for a few minutes Pankaj was oblivious of his surroundings.

The flashback was interrupted by his strong urge to go out and smoke. It is strange, he felt often that whenever such flashbacks happened to him, he felt an urge to smoke. Unlike his other colleagues who smoked, he never felt like smoking when he was under tremendous work pressure.

That happens to many of us who intend to smoke under lot of pressure. But the fact is that all this ultimately boils down to one's own psychology.

During his college days, Pankaj used to be a heavy smoker. He use to smoke atleast 20 cigarettes a day. But after he joined this profession, during the first year he saw atleast half a dozen journalists in their forties having massive heart attacks. Two of them survived, the rest couldn't. All of them were heavy smokers and had never learnt to say "no" to alcohol. They were like fixtures at the Press Club.

The two who survived, after recuperating, stopped coming to the Press Club. However, there was no dearth of people who were more than ready to replace them as 'fixtures' on the bar there. Incidentally most of such 'fixtures' at the Press Club bar are able to hold their drinks and also regularly pay for themselves.

They come, sit or stand at their favourite corners and keep on guzzling their vodkas and whiskeys without making any fuss and then quietly move out. However, what irritates many is that there are some regulars here who would make too much of noise, would get drunk, create trouble for everyone around.

Sameera touched his hand and he was jolted. A familiar touch, a soft and warm touch.

"Hey, are you alright?," she asked.

"Oh! I am just fine, I am fine."

"But your eyes are red. It seems you didn't sleep properly last night. What happened?," She was staring straight at his face looking deep into his eyes and Pankaj felt as if he has been caught red-handed.

He told himself, "I am screwed."

He promptly lied, "Oh, Yeah! I couldn't sleep properly, there was no electricity whole night, some local fault and the inverter stopped functioning after 2 a.m. in the night, so just couldn't sleep properly."

"You should have taken leave to take some rest during day."

Pankaj didn't know what to say. And he couldn't help but lie again, "I have an important assignment today. I can't afford to miss it." And he left.

❑

14

Love is not what you say to me.....

Pankaj had to tell her that he was in love with her. He was quite sure of this by now.

Nisha had to tell him that she was in love with him. She was quite sure of this by now.

How to do it? The idea of a formal proposal sounded bizarre to him. He felt he has grown up and greeting cards, e-cards, messages on mobile phone, lovey-dovey-emails, mushy stuffed toys were not the right way to express love.

"It is too childish. It is too clichéd. It is stupid and bizarre to express your love like this," he had always suggested to many of his friends who went ahead and used cards or toys to express their love for their girl friends.

Nisha was tired of the typical 'Mills and Boons' stories of her friends right from the school days and always felt that the expression of love has to be subtle, "Why does one need to express it? It just flows like the wind, like water in a river that flows through the heart of mountains. Whatever one feels can be heard only by this quiet and invisible river or the mountains. There is no need to interpret what a river says. It just moves ahead the way it has to and says what it has to without making a conscious effort. Love is like that, love has to be like that—calm, serene, ever flowing!"

She had long sessions of discussion with Lata about this in recent days and Lata had one day candidly quoted Mark Twain, "Love is the irresistible desire to be irresistibly desired."

"You see, this is the idea of love for most of the people. That is why they get possessive. But they don't realise this transforms love into a bondage and not an everlasting bond. Most of the relationships go haywire because of this possessiveness. Something that doesn't make you feel secure is not love. It is a desirc."

"May be this also happens because all of us are so insecure and when we fall in love then we become even more insecure as we do not want to lose a person who is so close to our heart. Gradually, this sense of insecurity becomes so over-powering that it starts getting expressed by way of possessiveness lovers show," Lata's lecture continued, "and initially, everyone likes it that someone is possessive about them, but then it becomes stifling. One feels suffocated. But there is only one end to this and that is—'break-up.'"

"The sooner it happens the better it is," Lata finally concluded her monologue which Nisha was hearing attentively.

"So that means every love relationship has to end in a disaster?," Nisha rolled the question towards Lata with a slight frown indicating she was somehow not convinced by Lata's theory.

"I never said that," Lata ducked the googly with slighty raised voice.

"All I am trying to tell you is......," she left her sentence halfway through and with a glee said, "Yup.....got it ...this is what I am trying to say..."

And then Lata fixed her gaze at the screen of her laptop and read from the screen, explaining the aftermaths of what happens when one gets possessive in love, "Love is like quicksilver in the hand. Leave the fingers open and it stays. Clutch it, and it darts away."

This one is by Dorothy Parker, she informed Nisha.

"And who the hell is Dorothy Parker?," Nisha mumbled irritatingly.

"Let us check baby, we have internet here which has answers to all such questions," Lata snapped her fingers while smiling at Nisha's irritation. She knew that her best friend was madly in love with Pankaj but refused to accept that because she was scared what would happen to her if he wasn't in love with her.

"Nisha you should go and have a heart to heart chat with Pankaj. You are in love with him and there is nothing wrong to tell him so," Lata just dropped the bomb like a 'silent killer'.

"No one is going to do it for you, you will have to do it yourself," she went on before Nisha could lodge a customary feeble protest over free and plenty of advice.

Meanwhile, Lata was ready with some interesting information about Dorothy Parker.

"Hey! This is interesting. Let me read it for you," Lata focused on the screen of laptop.

"According to Wikipedia, Dorothy Parker was an American poet, short story writer, critic and satirist, best known for her wit, wisecracks, and eye for 20th century urban foibles."

"Wow! That is interesting and before Nisha could look at her laptop or protest the way Lata was shifting discussion from one subjects to another as if she was dribbling in a hockey ground making Nisha feel more irritated, Lata had suddenly shut down the laptop."

She didn't give her anymore time to think and started firing questions at her as if she was hitting through the goal posts with series of penalty strokes.

"Why aren't you telling him?"

"Is he going around with someone else?"

"Did he tell you that he didn't like you?"

"Is he a flirt?"

"Are you not his type?"

Nisha didn't reply to any of these volleys and just got up informing Lata in a very cold voice and no nonsense tone, "I am going to make some hot tea, do you want some?"

"Of course, of course," Lata said and didn't make it obvious to Nisha that she had a sigh of relief as soon as Nisha said this. She didn't want her to look at the laptop while she was reading from Wikipedia about Dorothy Parker.

Why?

It was 2 a.m. when this question woke up Nisha who anyway was half-asleep thinking about how she should tell Pankaj that she was in love with him.

She quietly got up and switched on the laptop lying at a nearby table, connected internet and checked profile of Dorothy Parker and realised why Lata had suddenly shut down the laptop and didn't read further about Dorothy Parker's profile.

"Dorothy Parker had a conflicted and unhappy childhood," the sentence was staring from the screen at Nisha. She looked at Lata's innocent face with a weary smile, shut down the laptop, made a note of getting hold of some of Dorothy Parker's literary works as and when she gets a chance.

As she lied down on a floor bedding next to Lata, her eyes remained opened and she kept on staring at the ceiling which was not visible due to darkness all-around.

Dark thoughts of her unhappy and conflicted childhood rushed back to her. She didn't realise how long it took for her to sleep.

But surprisingly next morning when she woke up, everything was clear in her mind. "I am in love with Pankaj and I am going to tell him this today," she told herself. And there was smile on her face, she felt spring was in the air, she could smell roses.

She started getting ready. She looked at her mobile phone. "No New Messages" was the information relayed as she touched her finger on the "Messages" icon. She took a deep breath, stretched her body and got up from the bed to get ready. Lata was still sleeping.

Nisha got ready within an hour. During the night a slight drizzle ensured that the morning was pleasant. She could smell roses all-around and felt light as a feather as she moved with rapid strides towards Patel Nagar Metro Station.

She started humming a song by John Paul Young.

"Love is in the air
Everywhere I look around
Love is in the air
Every sight and every sound
And I dont know if I am being foolish
Don't know if I am being wise
But its something that I must believe in
And its there when I look in your eyes."

She was enjoying her own humming so much, probably the lyrics captured her mood perfectly! She didn't realise how many times she had repeated these lines. She was in a different world and came back to her real world only when she saw a long queue outside the security gate of the Patel Nagar Metro Station.

Two hours later, Pankaj got up and he had made up his mind that he can't continue like this. It was affecting his work. He must talk to Nisha and let her know that he loves her. "Even if she doesn't love me, it is fine, atleast I would know and can decide what to do with my life then? But it just can't continue like this," Pankaj told himself.

❑

15

Common! Say it Na☺

Pankaj had finally made up his mind how he is going to do this.

Nisha had decided that she is going to have a heart to heart talk with him.

She was excited. She was scared. She was not sure how Pankaj is going to react to this. She found him to be a quite a different kind of person. He was quite mature and didn't try to create false impression. She realised that she fell in love with him because he tended to underplay everything about himself. He didn't brag about himself and was a patient listener.

She was not sure that even if he loved her, was he ever going to say this to her. "He is too decent to make me feel uncomfortable about anything," she told herself. For the last three months they often walked to the Metro Station at Rajiv Chowk together and it was Nisha who was talking most of the time.

He listened to everything she said with a genuine interest and always encouraged her when she felt that the chips were down.

In fact both of them found great comfort in each other's company. Unlike what their friends often shared with them, it was not a roller coaster ride over the wheels of love. They longed to be in each other's company but they were not mad about this.

They had talked with each other about their families, friends, likes, dislikes and what not—everything they could think of.

As soon as Nisha entered the gym and reached her desk she switched on her computer and a message popped up from her Yahoo Messenger. She was surprised, it was too early for Pankaj to be in office. He must have sent it from his home, it was only 9:30 a.m. The message was even more surprising, "I have two movie tickets for Satyam Cineplex in Patel Nagar. This is for evening show of 6:30 p.m. to 9:30 p.m. Will you be able to come?"

Nisha smiled and without blinking twice or thinking even once replied, "Sure! But you will have to drop me back home as you know it not safe to walk down after 9:30 p.m. from the theatre to my home."

The reply came back instantly, "Gr8. See you at 6:15 p.m. at Satyam Cineplex. I won't be coming to office today as I have taken a compensatory off so I will meet you straight at Satyam."

Nisha replied back, "Sure! C ya @ 6:15 p.m."

Meanwhile the phone on her desk had started ringing. The first call she picked up was from a 'cold lead' which means a client she was pursuing for months but was not much hopeful for. This was one Mr. Girish Kumar, a businessman. He had called up to inform her that he had decided to take a membership package for his family of four—he himself, his wife and two daughters."

"I will send one of my office boys with a cheque. Just let me know the amount," he sounded like a man on mission.

Nisha had never felt so good in so many days. She had a date in the evening where she was going to say the most important one-liner which many of us get to say only once in a life time, "I love You."

And what a perfect start of this most important day of her life. "Wow! Business is booming. Luck is on my side today. Nothing can go wrong today, nothing!"

And then she didn't know what was happening. The phone just didn't stop ringing. By the time she was ready to have her lunch, she had booked 10 new clients for the gym. It was a record of sorts in this gym.

By the evening, she had booked five more. In one single day, she had generated a revenue of around Rs. 2 lakh for the gym. Everyone was congratulating her.

Dr. Tanya came to her in the evening at around 4:45 p.m. with a big beaming smile.

"Hey Nisha! What did you have in the breakfast this morning. From which side of the bed you got up. Lady luck is not just smiling on you, it is pulling out all stops to make you happy and rich."

Before Nisha could say anything, she had pushed a plain white envelope on her table with Nisha's name written on it.

"What's this?," Nisha asked, with a confusing look.

"Open it. Our owner has sent it for you after he got the news that you have broken all records of revenue generation which this gym has ever had," Dr. Tanya said.

Nisha opened the envelope. She almost screamed with joy, got up and hugged Tanya, "Thaaaaaaaanks Tanya."

What she had taken out of the envelope was a cheque of Rs. 10,000 with two letters of appreciation, one from the manager and the other one from the owner.

"You deserve it," Tanya hugged her even more tightly.

They stood there for few seconds like this. It is strange that at times when you achieve something you share your real joy with someone who is not so close to you, who is neither a relative, nor a member of the family. But you feel at that moment that this person is the closest to you.

"I am going to take a treat from you," Tanya said with a smile. Nisha added, "Of course, tell me, when do you want it."

"Let us go to CP after work today, I have nothing much to do, we can have a Pizza at Pizza Hut and do lot of window shopping," Tanya was quick to offer.

Nisha kept quiet and then with great difficulty told her, "Hey! Can we do it tomorrow. I have to meet a friend today in evening."

"And who is the lucky guy who is going on date with you," Tanya said with her trademark smile with a twinkle in her eye and dimples on her cheeks.

"No, No, it is not a date. It is just a friend...," Nisha was fumbling.

"Oh! Come on, the way you are blushing tell me that he is more than a friend," Tanya gave no respite to Nisha.

"OK! OK! If you think this is so, then let it be so," Nisha tried to get over this conversation. She realised, it was around 5 p.m. and she has to move out of office within next five minutes or she would not reach in time at Satyam.

"OK! Enjoy your date. See you tomorrow," Tanya said and moved away to her desk at reception.

Nisha was out of breath by the time she had managed to move out of office. She had just done some light make-up in the rest room meant for staff. She looked at herself for a few moments and was not sure whether she was looking as a girl should look for the day when she was going to confess her love to someone with whom she wanted to spend the rest of her life probably.

But she had little choice. It was 5:15 p.m. already and she was rushing to the Rajiv Chowk Metro Station.

She got her train at 5:35 P.M. Though the train was moving at the normal speed but after every station, Nisha would check her watch. By the time she had reached Rajendra Place Metro Station she had started getting nervous.

And she suddenly realised as the train came to a halt at Shadipur Metro Station, from where it takes five minute walk to reach Satyam Cineplex, that she didn't even know which movie they were going to watch.

Pankaj saw her coming from a distance. He was standing in front of Satyam Cineplex's entry gate smoking a cigarette.

She saw him taking the last few drags and then stubbing it before she reached there.

It was 6:05 p.m.

"Hi! How are you?," Pankaj started the conversation and offered her a chewing gum. He was wearing black jeans with a plain grey Tee shirt and sneakers. She was wearing blue jeans and white shirt with sneakers. Pankaj noticed that. "It is probably the same set of blue jeans and white shirt which she was wearing when I had met her for the first time in Metro." He couldn't recall whether she was wearing sneakers on that day or not.

"By the way, which movie we are going for?," Nisha wanted to ask but she stopped as she didn't want to sound stupid.

He heart was pounding and her mind had stopped working. She didn't want to look nervous and she had realised that she might not be able to say to him what she wanted to say. She felt like hugging him, there and then and whispering in his ear, "I love you."

But she realised, that was even a more stupid idea. There were conflicting thoughts in her mind.

Pankaj appeared very normal but he was very nervous too. He had never expected that Nisha would accept her invitation in the first place. He didn't know how he was going to tell her that he was in love with her.

Then as all first time lovers do, he also had thought of various options and then found this one to be the easiest one. The idea was that if she would refuse to come for the movie then it would simply mean that she is not interested in him at all and they would remain just good acquaintances. He had told himself that even if that happened he would be fine with that as she is a nice person and there is nothing wrong if she doesn't show any interest in him.

Both of them went quietly inside auditorium number two. As soon as they entered, it was pitch dark, the movie was just about to begin. On the big screen, promos of some of the upcoming films were being run. "Sorry, I didn't tell you earlier that the tickets are for" "*Janne Tu, Jaane Na.*"

Nisha was trying to look in the dark. A Cineplex employee holding a pencil torch was standing a few yards away and to reach them they had to go down the staircase in the auditorium. It was probably sheer instinct that she held Pankaj's hand. Pankaj was thankful to the darkness that no one could see his expressions. Nisha's touch was electrifying. There was warmth oozing out of her hand as she held Pankaj's hand and that warmth was enveloping not only Pankaj's body but his soul too.

Nisha, on the other hand, felt so safe and secure after so many years. She could feel that all that was pent up inside her heart and soul for so many years was just melting down. She just never wanted to leave that hand. She, too, was thankful to the darkness all around that no one could see the tears of joy in her eyes.

They tip-toed the staircase carefully and showed tickets to the man with the torch. He just murmured in a hardly audible voice, "H21 and H22." He threw the torch light for a split second to the "H" row in the auditorium and said, "corner one and the next to the corner Sir."

Pankaj replied, "Thanks" and holding hands, they walked towards the 'H' row of seats. There were not too many viewers in the auditorium. The movie was running here for the last two weeks. This was the beginning of the third week.

There were all kinds of viewers in the auditorium. Young couples, families with kids, bunch of college students.

Both Pankaj and Nisha slumped in their seats. While sitting they could not keep on holding each other's hand. As soon as they sat, the movie started.

Ten minutes into the movie, Nisha heard what she wanted to hear. Pankaj whispered in her ear, "Would you mind, if I hold your hand?".

"He is so sweet, so decent. He is so wonderful," Nisha thought.

Pankaj was surprised that he had never practiced this line while he was making plans to express Nisha to express his love for her. There was silence between the two for a few seconds.

And then Nisha, instead of replying to Pankaj, just placed her hand on Pankaj's hand. Her palms were a little sweaty. They were soft. But she held Pankaj's hand strongly. And before Pankaj could say anything or even react, he felt something heavy on his shoulders. Nisha had wrested her head on his shoulders.

For next one hour and 10 minutes before 'Interval' flashed on the big screen, Nisha didn't know what was going on the screen. She had just kept her eyes closed most of the time with her head wresting on his shoulders. In between whenever she opened the eyes, instead of looking at the movie screen she just looked at Pankaj's face.

Pankaj sat almost motionless. He just asked twice in between in whispering voice to Nisha, "Are you OK?" and then, "Are you comfortable?"

Every time he said this, the reply from Nisha was same, "Hmm.."

Pankaj too felt like closing his eyes and just Staying still. He was not able to think about anything else. That feeling of being so close to someone, especially the one whom you love, was amazing.

As soon as the lights came on during the interval, both of them got bolt from the blue and suddenly sat straight. They looked around without looking at each other. They were not holding hands now. They didn't want to catch people's attention without realising that there were atleast 25 couples in the auditorium who were sitting holding each other's hands.

Both of them took their turn to go the washrooms. Pankaj bought two Cans of soft drink and a pack of Popcorns. These things cost a bomb in multiplexes in Delhi. A soft drink Can, which normally costs around Rs. 30-35 in the market would cost no less than Rs. 60-70 in a multiplex and even a regular popcorn pack could cost almost 100 bucks. But when one is love struck, who cares about money?

Watching movies on a multiplex is probably a luxury which even the well-to-do middle class families in Delhi can afford only once in a while.

The movie started again in few minutes. Pankaj was holding the Popcorn packet. Both of them sipped soft drink from their cans and munched on the popcorn. In half an hour they had finished both. And then this time no one asked anything from anyone.

Nisha just kept her head on his shoulders again and Pankaj just held her hand tightly. He wanted to soak all the warmth which he was being surrounded by due to sheer presence of this simple yet extraordinary girl. Nisha just wanted the time to stop and sit like that till eternity.

Pankaj walked her down to her home after the movie. While coming back towards the metro station, he messaged her, “You looked wonderful as always☺.”

Nisha replied back within three seconds, “Luv u, Missing you already☺.”

❑

16

Six months later

Pankaj was on cloud nine. And why he shouldn't be? He had found his soul mate. He was one of the fortunate ones. Many of us feel that we have fallen in love. But the fact is that most of the times we perceive it as love. As someone starts caring about you, it is humane to fall for that person. So when someone cares about you, you feel that you are in love.

But then after sometime 'lovers' start fighting with each other. It starts with smaller fights, then it turns into cold wars and ego clashes which last for days turning into weeks and finally the saner and luckier ones realise that it is not working out and go for what you call "break-up." It breaks your heart for a moment, may be for few days or weeks or months but then the souls at least remain unscarred.

There are very few who find their soul mates in each other. It often happens that the guy or the girl may find a soul mate in their lover but is not necessary that the lover should find a soul mate in the same guy or the girl two. Thus, it could be a one way street and in fact many relations stink because of this.

But Nisha and Pankaj were realising that they were amongst very few, the chosen ones, who could find a soul mate in each other.

Ever since they had watched that movie together and realised that they were madly in love with each other, their routine had not changed much. The only difference was that they would often watch a movie and have a quiet dinner or a quick coffee in a restaurant or a coffee bar.

Pankaj realised that there was something special about Nisha. She was always ready to give him space. Many a times he had cancelled their rendezvous just hours before they were scheduled to meet as he had to go for an emergency assignment but Nisha never complained.

She would always say on such occasions with a smile, "I like your dedication to work. People like you are rare. Your work ethics are valuable and I want to help you to grow. So please go ahead and file a good story, I will read it in tomorrow's newspaper and let you know whether it was worth cancelling our dinner date or not."

Pankaj would just smile and he would try to write the best copy.

He had, incidentally, not told Sameera about what was happening between him and Nisha. He somehow felt deep inside his heart that Sameera might get hurt. He also realised that Sameera had something for him, it was more than friendship.

"You don't even look at me these days, do you realise how much weight I have lost and how beautiful I look these days, " Sameera would still chuckle with him with such casual looking but seriously intended remarks while they met during editorial meetings or in the news-room or over a cup of coffee in the canteen.

Nisha never called him during office hours, she would just message him once in while- "Missing you" or "Hope that we can go together in the evening, I will wait till you finish your office work."

Pankaj and Nisha would almost everyday walk down to Rajiv Chowk Metro Station together. They would board the same Metro. Sometimes when there would be too much rush, he would just suggest her, "You should go to the coach reserved for women, I will go in the other one."

Nisha would not say "No" to him but she didn't like travelling alone when Pankaj was with him.

Sameera would sometime accompany them too up to Rajiv Chowk Metro Station but then would take a different Metro. She could realise that there was something happening between Pankaj and Nisha and this bled her heart. But she would never let that reflect on her face or gestures. She was always 'ever smiling, never serious' Sameera.

She had casually asked Pankaj once in the office canteen, "Is there something going on between you and Nisha? She is a nice girl and you look good together. Just let me know who proposed whom ..." And Pankaj had politely cut the conversation in between, "There is nothing of that sort. You know that I would let you know about any such thing if it happens."

He said this with great pain as he knew he was lying to one of his best friends who probably loved him a lot too and had always stood by him.

He had never discussed these issues with Nisha also. Somehow Nisha never asked too many questions about anyone around Pankaj. She was happy to listen to whatever he told.

"You never ask too many questions. All my friends who are in love are always scared of their girlfriends who keep a hawk eye on them?," Pankaj asked her once.

"Why should I? You tell me what I need to know and all I know is that I love you and I trust you. I just think about you. I don't feel like asking anything from you. I just feel that I should be with you," Nisha replied.

Pankaj was speechless. Nisha had aksed him once, "You never asked about my past. Did I have any boyfriends etc.?" "Why should I?," Pankaj had reacted.

"Because most of the guys are like that. Within a week of starting a relationship, they start digging to find all that they want to know," Nisha said.

Pankaj shrugged his shoulders, "May be, I don't know. But I find this bizarre. I am OK with what I am and you are perfect for me the way you are. I don't feel like finding anything."

❑

17

Staying Awake!

"Hello Beta! How are you? I need to talk to you. Can you come to Chandigarh for a day or two?"

Nisha was listening to her father's voice. The tone was quite soft and compelling too.

"What happened Papa? Are you OK?"

"Yes I am fine *Beta*. But I need to talk to you."

"About what Papa? You can tell me on phone."

"No *Beta*, it cannot be told on phone."

Silence.

Neither Nisha responded nor her father for a few seconds.

"Are you there Nisha?," the silence broke with her father's voice.

"Yes Papa, I am listening…"

She hesitated for a few seconds. Somehow she neither wanted to prolong the conversation, nor did she want to go to Chandigarh. She couldn't make out what was happening, what made her father call her back home when he knew that she was least interested in going back and spending time with him.

"Is Shekhar OK?," Nisha asked in a little worried voice.

"Yes, he is fine. Don't worry, there is no problem here, it is just that I want you to come back home for a few days as there are some important issues that need to be discussed."

Nisha responded, trying her best to avoid going to Chandigarh, "I will have to check with my manager Papa, this is peak season and I might not get leave."

The voice on the other end stiffened. And he spoke like as many fathers do to their grown up kids at times, "You have to come. If you can't then let me know by this evening and I will come to Delhi myself. This is something so important that it cannot wait."

Nisha realised that this time there is no getting away from going back home, so she surrendered but not without giving herself a last chance, "OK Papa, I will apply for leave today and let you know by this evening when I can come."

"I want you back home by this weekend, you just have to take one day leave on Saturday as Sunday is your weekly off and you can join your office back on Monday. I will wait for your call this evening."

Before Nisha could say anything further, she could hear the long beep sound that told her that the phone had been disconnected by the caller at the other end.

She took a deep breath and checked her watch, "It was 7 a.m. and the day was Tuesday."

A bad beginning for a day about which she was excited as Pankaj had told her that he had got tickets for a new Bollywood film and they had planned to go to a newly opened Japanese restaurant in Connaught Place after that.

They met in the evening near Plaza cinema hall. The film to be screened was Salman Khan starrer "Dabang". It was around 6 p.m. The movie was supposed to start at 6:30 p.m. Pankaj had to file a couple of stories from the press releases and he was free by 5:30 p.m.

"Going on a date?," Sameera had asked her as he was switching off his computer and hurriedly trying to get out of office without realising that Sameera was standing just behind his chair.

"What do you think?," he chuckled.

"Well, well! reporters are not paid to think but to find hard facts," Sameera quipped.

"You know, I can't hide anything from you. I don't know whether you call it a date or just going out for a movie with a friend," Pankaj remarked sheepishly while picking up his bag.

A small whistle escaped Sameera's glossy lips reflecting the touch up she had done just a few minutes ago in the office restroom.

"Not bad, Dude! Go and enjoy the evening!," she said while sitting on her chair and switching on the desktop in one swift motion.

"And by the way say my hi to Nisha," she said nonchalantly.

"Oh come on, how do you know I am going out with Nisha," Pankaj lamely tried to counter.

Sameera swung her chair and with a piercing stare at Pankaj's face dropped the punch line, "There are two things which made me say this buddy, one, I am a reporter and I am trained to find information which people do not intend to reveal and two, apart from me she is the only other young woman in your life. So if you are not going out with me, you are obviously going out with her and by the way your story on corruption in the civic bodies has created quite a furore in power corridors, so next time you visit office of any of the civic bodies, be careful as someone might try to even kill you," Sameera said with a smile which had strange mix of warmth and sarcasm, sweetness and a sense of loneliness.

"No one can win from you Sameera, you are the best," he patted her on shoulder and left.

"How did you manage the tickets?" Nisha asked the same question she would ask every time whenever they went out for a blockbuster movie. I had checked online and there were notickets available.

Pankaj would give the same reply, "Oh! I just requested one of the crime reporters and he spoke to the area police-station in-charge. They are good friends, so the tickets were delivered by one of the constables last evening. " Nisha just loved to look at Pankaj while he tried to be as modest as he could. "Hmmm…it is good to love a journalist, you are never going to miss out a movie if you want to watch it," she chuckled.

"Oh! Common Nisha, don't pull my leg. It is just that I am lucky to have some friends who are at the right place."

"Oh really! But I think you too have some good contacts. I read your story exposing corruption in civic bodies today. How do you get so much of information?," Nisha was inquisitive as always.

"Remember…. No office talk when we are out. It is should be just about you and me," Pankaj reminded her of one of "commandments" both of them had put together over a period of six months in an effort to ensure that they don't end up fighting and complaining and hence crushing a beautiful relationship even before it has blossomed.

"*Ok…baba*…no office talk, but I have to tell you something important," Nisha said, nibbling on a black forest pastry as Pankaj sipped a butter scotch flavoured milkshake from typically shaped glass bottle. They had bought it from one of the oldest confectionary outlets in Connaught Place, "Caventers."

Both of them liked to come here for the simplicity of the shop. People throng this outlet in hundreds everyday. The prices are very reasonable. There is a small counter over which you can buy sandwiches, patties, cold coffee, flavoured milk and have them while standing there.

The ambience of Caventers and the area surrounding it where all the customers stand and enjoy their snacks or milk shakes always mesmerised Pankaj. On the surface, there was nothing much to say. But unlike dozens of restaurants lined up around this simple snacks shop, here one found people at ease with themselves. You would find old couples reliving the glorious past of Central Delhi standing there and sipping strawberry shake whereas you could always see young kids from the nearby schools full of exuberance oozing out of the bantering they would indulge in with their friends.

Nisha knew that Pankaj liked this place a lot. So whenever she got a chance, she would always suggest herself that both of them should go to that place. Over the last six months or so they had almost tasted everything on the menu and had liked most of them.

"So what do you want to tell me?," Pankaj said lighting a cigarette. Nisha didn't like the fact that he smoked but didn't object to it. She had told herself, "I don't want to behave typically like those girls who start objecting to smoking and drinking of guys with whom they fall in love. They will change on their own. Men are men. And this is how they behave."

She had realised that Pankaj was not very demanding but he needed to have his own space and he had always respected her space also. That was probably one reason that they hadn't picked up a fight with each other even once ever since they fell in love.

"My father called up this morning, he wants me to come to Chandigarh this weekend."

"Anything serious? I hope everything is well. Your dad is OK? "

Both of them had reached entrance of Plaza and were about to enter.

"We will talk about this after the movie. I need to talk to you in detail," Nisha said.

"OK," Pankaj said with a frown.

During the movie, Nisha was unusually quiet with her head on Pankaj's shoulders.

Pankaj also didn't disturb her. Infact during the intermission also, she told Pankaj not to leave his seat and be there. She said she didn't want anything and just want him to be close to him.

It was a little strange behaviour. But Pankaj didn't say anything. "Women are women and they behave like that," he told himself.

After the movie, Nisha suggested, "Let us not go to the restaurant for dinner, we can get something packed and we can eat at my place."

Pankaj was little taken aback, "But what about Lata?,"

"She is not here. She has gone to Bhopal for a day for an interview. She would be back only tomorrow."

"OK, No issues. Let us go," Pankaj said moving towards parking where he had parked his car.

They reached at her Patel Nagar house in half an hour.

Pankaj parked his car in front of the house which had stairs from outside. Both of them climbed to the second floor. It was 110 sq. yard accommodation with two big rooms, a small room, kitchen and a bathroom.

The girls had kept it nice and clean and though there was hardly any furniture worth mentioning, the house was tastefully done.

"It is very tastefully done," Pankaj said.

"Thanks, Nisha said, while she showed him the house".

"You know both me and Lata have separate rooms but she would always come to my room in the middle of the night and wake me up. "She is too scared to be sleeping alone at night." So every night, we end up sleeping in one room, sometimes, it is mine, sometimes it is hers."

Both of them had decided that they would order a Domino's Pizza after reaching Nisha's place as that would spare them the hassle of getting food packed on the way.

"Would you like to have some tea, coffee, soft drink?,"

"I will have something cold," Pankaj said. He was sweating less because of the room temperature but more because of the fact that he realised he was alone in this house with such a beautiful girl whom he loved and adored.

Nisha opened the refrigerator, opened a bottle of Coke and poured into two glasses.

She flipped on the TV switch, tossed remote control set to Pankaj while telling him, "You can watch some television, while

I will order Pizaa. She had the number of local Domino's outlet in her mobile phone address book."

She knew that Pankaj didn't like cheese toppings and always preferred to eat the simplest Pizza. So she ordered one large sized onions and capsicum Pizza. She knew it could be too big for the two of them but then she could always preserve some in the refrigerator for the next day.

That is the best thing about Pizzas, if you have a refrigerator and there is no power cut, not even a crump of pizza would ever go waste."

They had their pizza and the coke and they snuggled together. Nisha could feel the warmth of his body and Pankaj enjoyed the softness of her hands. They just looked into each other's eyes and then kissed.

Nisha enjoyed the warm touch of his lips while she held him tight. Pankaj now realised why this cliché of a girl's fingers in the guy's hair as a romantic motif is so popular. He was in a different world and so was she.

And then the mobile ringer shrieked. With a sudden jolt both of them pulled away from each other. But the best thing was they were comfortable with what they had done. They were not embarrassed.

Nisha saw the number flashing on her phone. It was a call from her father. She had somehow forgotten that she had to leave for Chandigarh this weekend and talk to Pankaj about this in detail too as she had an intuition that something bizarre is going to happen.

"Yes Papa, she picked up the phone?"

"Where were you? How come you took such a long time to pick up the phone?"

"I was here Papa,...(pause)..at home, what happened, why are you sounding so worked up? I hope everything is all right?," She sensed that somehow her father could know sitting 300 kms away that her daughter was with someone at this point of time.

But she was cool about this and her conversation in no way betrayed any panic even if that was written all over her face.

"I hope you are coming to Chandigarh this weekend as we had discussed," he said.

"Yes, I am, I will let you know whether I am coming by train or bus."

"Where is Lata?," his parting question came back to her hurled like grenade.

"She will be latc tonight?"

"Hmmmm……" followed by the sound which informed that the phone has been disconnected from the other side.

"What happened?," Pankaj was trying to act normal, though he was not. He just wanted to hold her and kiss again.

"I forgot to tell you that I have to go to Chandigarh for this weekend," Nisha said.

"Is everything OK?," Pankaj frowned.

"Don't know! Papa called up earlier this morning and just told me that I should be there.

"I hope he is not getting you married," Pankaj said with an attempted faint smile.

Nisha looked at him with a strange melancholic look, came forward, took his hands in hers and before Pankaj could say anything put her on lips on his. Pankaj felt the warmth turning into heat, they kissed.

Again a jolt with sound of "beep, beep". It was a message from Pankaj's mother. "When are you coming?," Pankaj realised that it was almost past midnight.

"I should leave now, it is late," he got up from the floor bedding.

Nisha gave him a warm hug and whispered in his ears, "Love You, Be close to me always." Pankaj could feel the rush of blood in his head with his temples throbbing.

He didn't know how to react, he just hugged her and told her, "Love you too."

"Message me when you reach home," "Nisha said as Pankaj stepped out of the door."

"Sure, I will," he said.

After an hour, a message flashed on her cell phone, "Reached. You looked beautiful today, as always, luv u."

Nisha's fingers promptly punched the mobile keypad and within 15 seconds the reply was flashing on Pankaj's cell phone screen with a smiley, "Miss u sweetheart. Give me a wake up call tomm., want to get up listening to your voice."

Pankaj didn't realise that Nisha would be awake whole night, thinking about the moments of passion between them. Pankaj too had trouble in sleeping and he was sleeping in bits and pieces.

❑

18

Upside Down!

In few minutes the world can go upside down for anybody. It can be anybody! It doesn't matter how many good deeds you have done or how many vices you have had, when the change comes, it often comes in a stormy way and doesn't leave much room for manoeuvring.

Delhi-Kalka Shatabdi halts at Chandigarh Railway Station. The train almost gets empty on this station. It leaves in the morning from New Delhi Railway Station.

Purushottam Lal was waiting just in front of the place meant for C-1 coach. A small metallic board hung from the ceiling by two iron rods on the platform in a series of many other such installations from the beginning upto the end of the platform. In bold yellow letters, one could see C-1 written on the board.

"I don't know how I am going to greet her and how I am going to convince her for what I want her to do. It won't be easy," he told himself.

His life had too many rough edges and he didn't blame anyone. His wife was physically beyond his reach as she had quietly decided to leave for the heavenly abode after a prolonged illness 10 years ago.

His two children were beyond his emotional reach too for reasons he couldn't share with anyone. The son and the daughter too found it impossible to share these reasons which had cut them off emotionally from their father.

Man is mortal probably because of his desires. If we hadn't have any desires, we too would be immortal perhaps. Desires are like a tiger, you may be able to decide when you would start riding them, but once you have begun this journey, it is the tiger which decides when you would get down. And it often happens that by the time one is able to get down, if one is lucky enough during the life time which many of us are not, one could be so weary, that all that is left of life are a few leftover pieces. One can't make anything out of it and one just starts waiting to get over all this. There is no time to go back and relive the life in a better way. One may rue this, but that is the way it is. Ironically, most of us realise it when it is already too late.

Purushottam also didn't know how it all happened, He was happily married to Saroj, a young well educated woman from Ambala, a place known for having an Indian Army cantonment. Saroj's father was a cloth merchant and Purshottam's father was a school teacher. Both of them lived in Ambala as their families had moved there from Lahore after India was divided in 1947 into two nations—India and Pakistan.

It was an arranged marriage between the two in 1985. By that time Purushottam had joined Chandigarh Administration as an upper division clerk. He was hardworking and street smart and his rise within the administration was swift. They had managed to buy a small house in Chandigarh and were living happily after the birth of their two children. By that time he was deputy director of the education department.

Then the tragedy struck. His son Shekhar was around 14 and daughter Nisha was 12 years old. Saroj fell unconscious one Sunday morning in the kitchen. He rushed her to PGI Chandigarh, a well-known government hospital. She stayed there for a couple of days. Several tests were conducted. She was discharged after two days. But the real tragedy struck when Purushottam got a call from one of the senior doctors.

"It is important that you come and meet me today," Dr. Naresh Dhingra told him courteously. Due to his position in the Chandigarh Administration, Purushottam had started enjoying some clout which got manifested in many ways. This courteous call from a senior doctor from one of the most prestigious health institutions in the northern India was one of the manifestations of this clout.

Purushottam cancelled his meetings and reached the hospital in 20 minutes flat. Those days Chandigarh was not as crowded and one could easily reach anywhere in the city in maximum half an hour.

Purushottam was crest fallen when the doctors told him that his wife had been diagnosed with "Cancer."

Life changed quickly after that. Saroj, kept on falling sick often and he was hard pressed to take care of the household chores and the children.

He felt emotionally drained more than often. He couldn't take it more and then in one of the inspection tours at one of the government schools, he happened to meet Neena Munjal. She had that serene look on her face and was a brilliant award winning teacher. She was in early thirties and a divorcee, living alone.

Purushottam doesn't remember how it happened, but somehow they kept in touch and one evening when he was feeling completely burnt out from the pressures of life, he just called her and asked her, "Can I come to your house and spend some time with you.".

That night he didn't go home and slept there with Neena in his arms. In the morning when both of them got up, none of them had any feelings of guilt. They felt they were soulmates.

Purushottam found the elixir of life which he thought he had lost. He remembered telling Nina one evening as she was sitting and having tea with her, "You know, one of the reasons I enjoy being with you is that you never make any demands, you don't say that you want to marry me. I hope that you never feel that I look at you like a mistress."

"Do you love me?," Nina asked

"I don't know, I am too unstable emotionally ever since my wife fell sick, I can't say."

She listened to his reply, got up, came close to him and hugged him tight. He felt secure and warm and emotionally content. That was all he wanted.

Nina never called him at his home or office. But then one day she was sick, she was alone and she was feeling utterly miserable.

She called him up at his home on his landline and while Purshottam was consoling her and assuring her that he would come soon to her house to be with her, his daughter unintentionally picked up an extension line to call up one of her friends. She was dumbfounded as she listened to the whole conversation.

That was the end of bonhomie between the daughter and the father. She never said anything to him about that conversation till her mother was alive but ever since that day she somehow didn't forgive him.

She kept the secret to herself till her mother passed away a couple of years later and then confronted her father. Purushottam told her to shut up and left the room. His relationship with Nina continued.

Shekhar came to know about this too and took the first opportunity to move out of city to study in an engineering college. He hated his father for betraying his mother when she was alive, more so after she had passed away. He missed her terribly. The more he cried thinking of his mother, the more he hated his father.

But the brother and sister jelled very well. That was the only solace for both of them.

The train came to a screeching halt. She had a small suitcase and a leather ladies bag hung casually on her shoulder. She was wearing black jeans and grey sweatshirt. Her hair were tied in a bun and the aftermath of getting very early in the morning was visible on her face.

Purushottam waved his hand but then brought it down with a feeling of embarrassment. Afterall his daughter was standing only half a metre away from her.

"Hi, Papa!," Nisha said with a visibly great effort to control herself, she just wanted to turn around and get into the train compartment again.

Her father, with brooding shoulders and a half-baked smile with a slight reflection of shrewdness stood in front of her. "You have lost weight, are you not eating properly," The favourite tagline of all parents for their children living away from them was how he greeted her.

"No, I am fine, I eat properly," a short and crisp reply from her.

Pause....

A few seconds passed.

"Let's go home," Purushottam broke the heavy silence and started walking towards the nearest exit gate at the platform.

While walking he took out the mobile phone from his right hand side trouser pocket and called up his driver.

By the time they covered the distance from the exit gate of the platform to the exit gate of the station, a steel grey coloured Ford Fiesta was waiting for them.

The biggest difference between cars in Chandigarh and Delhi is the number of scratches and dents. In Chandigarh one hardly find any scratches on the fenders or front guards of cars, they always look brand new while in Delhi one hardly finds a car without a scratch or a small dent. A five year old car in Chandigarh looks much younger than an year old car from Delhi!

It is cool to drive on Chandigarh roads, so Cool! This despite the fact that the old timers now-a-days rue that there is too much traffic in Chandigarh also and the city is losing its character.

But ask a Delhiite or a Mumbaikar and you would come to know the almost spiritual feeling they get even with an idea of driving on Chandigarh roads.

"And yet my father keeps a driver, there is no need for it, he is paying him from his own pocket," Nisha thought and then realised that she had decided long back that she wouldn't trouble herself by trying look at actions of her father through lens of logic.

After all what could explain the extra marital affair he had with Nina. She suddenly felt depressed as her past and her father's past came rushing back to her.

Her thoughts came to a halt as the car reached their house spread over around 300 sq. yards with a small garden each at back and front of the house.

Two garden chairs were sitting ideally looking at the table in between as if all three were looking for a family to sit together for years and they had lost all hope.

One just has to realise that often the things we call non-living could have their own expressions too!. Sounds unbelievable? Try it. Look at the things around you today and keep on looking at them everyday with different moods and feelings and you would realise that you can sense their mood too at times. After all every matter has some sort of energy. Isn't it?

❑

19

What the Hell!

"I don't believe this Papa, what the hell is this, you can't play with my life like this," Nisha's agony was getting reflected between sobs and flashes of anger.

"I think, I know what is best for you. I am your father and I would never do anything which would go against your interest and you dare not talk like this to me," the same old cliché was blurted out by Purushottam.

They were sitting in their living room which had a table made of glass, not too big but big enough to satisfy a Punjabi's ego who has done well in life. The upholstery was modest and the walls were decorated with handicrafts. An LED screen was tucked away at one of the walls. Purushottam loved to watch day-night cricket matches with his single malt whiskey at this LED screen.

The argument had begun half an hour back. It was one of those scenes which must be getting enacted and re-enacted in so many homes across the country everyday. The father or the parents fixing up the marriage of a young girl without taking her permission. Any protest from the girls are looked down upon by the elders in the family.

Half-an-hour back which was around one hour after Nisha had landed at her house, her father had shocked her when he told him that he had fixed up her match. The boy he had chosen was the son of one of their distant relatives. He was a junior engineer in Public Works Department (PWD) of Chandigarh.

He had shown her his photograph and asked, "What do you think? I think he is very handsome?"

"I am not interested in getting married. I want to make a career and then look at marriage Papa," she had politely but firmly informed him.

"His family is very open-minded, they do not have a problem if you would continue to work even after marriage," he tried to counter his daughter's move as if he was expecting this argument from her.

"I just don't want to get married Papa, atleast let me live my life the way I want to live for a couple of years," she told him again.

His tone and tenor changed. As very often parents do, by changing the tone and tenor, they send the message without saying it clearly, "No more discussions, we have taken enough sh***t from you. Now you will do what we tell you to do."

To hell with all that parental love on which they take pride. Children don't have a say beyond a point in most Indian families even after they turn 18 and parents often ironically are biggest icons of hypocrisy.

Purushottam too was no different from millions of Indian fathers. He dictated to Nisha, "There is no point in discussing too much about all this. I have fixed up your match. The engagement is tomorrow."

"What the hell, what the hell….," she was screaming and tears were rolling down her eyes. "You can't do this to me," …. She was also realising gradually that she was helpless.

"They will come tomorrow afternoon to meet you. Sandeep will also be there. It is just a formality. You two will exchange the rings after they come here and formally approve the match. You can talk to Sandeep separately when they come. We all will leave the two of you alone," he was telling her and Nisha was dumbfounded.

"How could, how could he do that....First he ruined my mother's life by sleeping with that damn woman. While his wife was dying, he was enjoying his escapades with that woman. He might be my father, but he is really a demon for me, I just cannot allow him to destroy my life?," She just wanted to blast him.

But before she could say anything he had just moved out of the living room leaving her alone to think about all this.

Her mind had started working furiously. She didn't have much time. The first call she placed was to her Shekhar. "The mobile number you are calling is out of coverage area," she got this message and then realised that he had informed her two weeks back that this weekend he will be going for trekking near Pindari glacier and it would not be possible to contact him on mobile or email for atleast a week.

The next person she called was Lata. She listened to her patiently, calmed her down and asked her, "So, Nisha, what do you want to do?"

"I don't know that exactly but I know one thing that I do not want to get married to this bloody Sandeep."

"And why is that, you haven't even met him?," Lata asked.

Nisha was furious by now.

"Lata, what the hell, you are on my side or on the other side?"

"I am on your side Nisha," Lata said in a cold voice. "And right now you are in a state that you are not thinking logically. I am just trying to help you realise that you need to have a good reason for not accepting what your father is telling you because this could mean a permanent break up of ties between you and your father. So you bloody well have a good reason for that so that you don't regret your decision later."

Nisha calmed down. "You are right."

"Lata, I am sure I do not want to get married to the guy my father has chosen for me because I want to spend my life with Pankaj. I love him and he loves me too and I think he is the best guy for me."

"Good! Nisha, that's better. That is a pretty good and sound reason for you to tell your father that you are not accepting his choice."

"Now tell me, will Pankaj marry you?,"

"Yes he should, why not?"

"No Nisha, please no assumptions on this count. You don't know guys. You better ask them."

"But Lata, I never thought like this. I trust him. Marriage is the logical end of being in love."

"Not necessarily," Lata argued. "He might be looking for a live-in relationship rather than getting married."

"Oh Come on Lata! You also know he is not like that," Nisha was amazed at Lata's arguments.

"Nisha, I don't know much about him and I would suggest that if you haven't asked Pankaj, you call him right now and ask him that whether he would marry you and when he will do that and if you are convinced about his answers, then go and tell your father that you are going back to Delhi and never coming back to him as you have decided that you will take care of your life now."

"And what if he says NO," Nisha asked in a trembling voice. She was on the verge of crying now. What a nasty mess she had landed in!

"Then it is good for you that you were not pegging your life on someone who was not going to spend the rest of the life with you. And if you are still sure after this about your decision of not getting engaged and ultimately being married to this bloody Sandeep, then it is better that you still tell your father that you are walking out. Take the first possible bus to Delhi, give me a call and I will be waiting for you at the ISBT (Inter States Bus Terminal at Kashmere Gate where all the buses coming from Chandigarh end their journey)".

"Don't worry Nisha, I am with you. You are not alone."

These words came like a soothing balm to Nisha and she felt again the surge of confidence. She was not alone after all!

She picked up her phone and dialled Pankaj's number. "The mobile number you have dialled is busy. Please wait for sometime or call again later," she heard the recorded voice and cursed Pankaj for a moment for talking so much on phone. Most of the time she called up, his phone was busy. That is the problem with journalists, they can't ignore any call. Even those from unidentified numbers cannot be ignored. You never know who is going to tip you off for the story of your life.

But sometime this could also change the story of your life. Pankaj would realise it much later though!

A scream full of agony.........!!!!

"Thud", sound of a body falling on floor.

She rushed outside.

Purushottam was lying flat on the porch.

Within no time, she realised her father had a heart attack.

"Oh my god!" she just whispered to herself.

She screamed and called the maid who was working in kitchen preparing the meal. The maid, Sharmila, came rushing and almost fainted when she saw Purushottam lying on the ground unconscious and Nisha standing with a pale face.

Nisha suddenly turned into live wire and came out of the slumber caused by sudden shock. "Sharmila, give me a hand, I have to take him to Hospital."

Sharmila was young but very strong and the two of them lifted Purushottam and put him on the back seat of the car. "Sharmila, you stay at home, I am going to hospital," Nisha didn't wait to answer for Sharmila's reply and raced to living room. The car keys were on the glass table at the centre of the room. She picked them up, almost jumped into the driving seat and started the car. She drove like a mad. PGI Hospital was 20 minutes drive from their house, she covered it in eight minutes flat and stopped the car just in front of the emergency gate.

❑

20

The last wish

22 Missed Calls and 13 Messages from Pankaj.

Nisha was sitting in corridor of the PGI Hospital outside the Intensive Care Unit when she looked at her mobile phone and realised Pankaj was frantically trying to contact her. She had kept her cell phone on silent mode all the time ever since she entered the hospital.

"It is good that you brought him in time. Had he not reached here for another five minutes, anything could have happened," Dr. Rakesh Nijhawan told her.

"Your father has suffered a massive heart attack. He is in critical state but we hope to do our best. You call any of your relatives you have here," he told her.

She almost mechanically asked, "Will he be OK doctor?"

Dr. Nijhawan looked at the brave girl standing in front of him with tears visible in her eyes. He patted her on shoulder, "We are doing our best. Let us wait for next 24 hours."

Nisha called up a few of her relatives who were in Chandigarh including his mother's sister. Their families had not been in much touch ever since her mother had passed away as Purushottam gradually got too involved with Nina finding solace in her company and shedding the rest of the relations around him after Saroj had died.

They came rushing to the hospital and consoled Nisha. One of her cousins, Nilesh, whom she was meeting after five years, was now in college. As Nisha's aunt stayed back at the hospital for the night along with her husband, Nilesh drove her back to home in late evening and decided to stay at their house for the night as Sharmila had to leave for her home.

They didn't talk much. Nilesh ordered some food from outside and both of them had a quiet dinner though Nisha could hardly eat.

It was strange, two cousins sitting together and eating. They didn't had much to talk.

She quietly got up, collected the dishes, dumped them in the kitchen and went to a room adjoining his father's bedroom.

Nisha suddenly felt she was exhausted. She just wrote a common mobile message to Pankaj and Lata. "My father is not well. I am taking care of him. He is in hospital. I will call you as soon as I can."

Before she could manage to read the responses, she just fell asleep with the mobile phone automatically getting switched off as its battery power had been exhausted too.

She suddenly woke up drenched in sweat. She had watched a dreadful dream and realised that she had slept without even switching on the fan. She saw the time on a wall clock hanging in front of her. It was 5:30 a.m. in the morning.

She went to the attached bathroom, washed her face.

No phone calls during the night. Good. It means the father is doing fine.

One really dreads the ring of a phone in the middle of the night or in wee hours when a dear one is in hospital.

She took time to get ready for going to hospital. As she walked out, after taking a bath and putting on some fresh clothes, Nilesh was sitting wide awake on a sofa watching television with the volume being put on mute mode.

"Let's go to hospital," she said.

It was 6:15 a.m.

He quietly picked up the car keys. Nisha locked the house and both of them reached PGI in 20 minutes. Nilesh was driving.

In this hour of the morning, traffic was hardly visible on Chandigarh roads. There were, though, large number of morning walkers. She looked through the side screen and realised that for all of them it is just another routine day. They are recharging themselves with the walk and exercises to take full advantage of the opportunities which they expect to come across during the day. But for her, it was an extended nightmare. She was feeling emotionally impoverished.

They reached the hospital.

One of her distant uncles was visibly relieved to see that she had come well in time so that he can go back home and start his day.

But before the uncle went, he handed over her a wad of notes. "These are Rs. 10,000 you may need them," he said quietly slipping the wad in her hand.

"She protested in a feeble voice, I have the money."

The uncle did not budge. "Keep it, keep it…"

She slipped the wad in her small handbag and started looking for the doctor on duty.

This was a lady doctor named Dr. Rekha Krishnan.

"How is Mr. Purushottam Lal doing?" she asked as she saw Dr. Rekha coming out of the ICU. Bleary eyed Dr. Rekha replied in a dry voice, "He is stable. He has regained consciousness this morning. It is a good sign. "

Both of them were talking while walking. Dr. Rekha was in a hurry to reach back her home after finishing the night duty.

Nilesh made Nisha go to the PGI canteen and have a cup of tea and two toasts.

He told her that he would keep a watch near ICU if there is a call from any of the doctors.

Nisha was back in twenty minutes. She told Nilesh to go back home as he had to go to college. She told him quietly while he was leaving the hospital premises, "Thanks a lot, Nilesh." He just noded his head and walked out as if feeling embarrassed for being thanked.

She sat there alone for half an hour. Pankaj must be asleep, she was thinking. She didn't want to wake him up with such a bad news. So much had happened over the last 24 hours that she would find it difficult to explain over the phone. Moreover, she was still feeling emotionally exhausted and was not in a mood to talk much about what was happening around her.

She flipped open her mobile phone and wrote a message to her brother informing him about his father's situation, but then deleted the message thinking that this would create lot of panic. She simply wrote a message, "Pl. call whenever you see this message. I am waiting for your call. Take care." and sent it to her brother's mobile phone. He will get to read this message as soon as he will switch on his mobile phone and get connected to the mobile network.

Another half an hour was spent with her aunt asking about her job in Delhi, where she lived and how did she manage herself. For a change despite being a home maker in a typical Punjabi joint family, her aunt was quite an open-minded person. She appreciated the kind of initiative she had taken by staying in Delhi and working there.

The hands of wrist watch tied on Nisha's wrist struck 8 a.m. and someone outside the ICU called, "Who is with Purushottam Lal?"

Nisha almost raced to reach near the ward boy who was almost screaming, "Is there anyone with Purushottam Lal?"

"I am with him, I am his daughter."

The ward boy looked at her and with a non-chalant look asked her, "He wants to see you. You only have few minutes".

She followed him inside the ICU. But before she could enter the main ward of ICU, she had to wear a special robe which was apparently made bacteria-free by carefully disinfecting it She had to take off her shoes and socks too.

She washed her hands with a special liquid soap kept on one corner of a washbasin in a plain unmarked bottle.

He was on bed number 6. It was a shock to see him. He had shrunk dramatically and looked as a caricature of his earlier self. And all this change had happened in just last 22 hours. Nisha stood by his side. He opened his eyes. His mouth and nose were covered with the transparent mask under which she could see lengthy, slim, cord like surgical tubes carrying oxygen and medicines to his body. On the back of the bed was a monitor where skewed lines continued to appear without any break showing his vital statistics.

He said it with his eyes and she didn't know how she understood that indication. She took herself close to his mouth so that she could listen if he had anything to say.

He whispered with great effort, "Promise me….you will marry Sandeep."

Nisha was dumbstruck.

She tried to get away and pretend that she had not listened to what he had said. "This is my last wish," he whispered.

She could see a drop of tear rolling down from the corner of his eyes. Suddenly that bond of paternity had viciously taken over her heart and mind. And she said "I Promise", without blinking twice.

He closed his eyes. And another drop of tear rolled down. This time from Nisha's eyes.

❑

21

This is Absurd! This is Life.

Last evening Pankaj had called her up 22 times and sent 13 text messages on her mobile phone asking her, urging her and ultimately pleading her to call him back.

Everyone has a sixth sense. Some listen to that, other's don't. Somehow, all of us have a premonition of the extraordinary events that influence our life permanently. These premonitions make us uncomfortable. We realise it. Whether we accept it or not is a matter of individual choice.

Pankaj's sixth sense was telling him, something is not right. Never before Nisha had behaved in such a strange way. Initially he was worried then he got irritated that she was not responding to his messages and calls. A couple of hours later he was overpowered by this strong and miserable feeling of helplessness.

"I am worried about Nisha. Her father is not well and she is not responding to my messages," Pankaj told Lata when he called her up next day to find whether she knew anything more about the situation in Chandigarh than what he knew. By this time he had got Nisha's message that her father was unwell. That made him even more worried. He desperately wanted to speak to her.

Lata did not share with him any details of how Nisha's father was pestering her to get married to Sandeep. It was a talk that two friends shared and she didn't want to breach the trust. Lata was not sure how Nisha would feel if she told Pankaj about the conversation they had. This is irritating for most guys that they don't get to know all that they feel they need to know. The girls, however, often feel that they need not share everything. They want to keep their own secrets, though in a harmless way. But this often ends up hurting the guys. Many a relationships start going haywire because of these complex response mechanism of girls. Atleast they find it complex, though girls have a different viewpoint.

Pankaj requested her to inform him as soon as gets to know anything more. For a moment he thought that he should go to Chandigarh and check out himself whether she needs his help but then dropped the idea. This could complicate the situation as Nisha might not be comfortable.

Sameera was on leave. She had gone out on a three day trip to Ajmer Sharif with two of her friends and would be back only couple of days later. Pankaj was starting to have a headache. He had not slept properly last night, being worried about Nisha.

Thankfully, the newsfall was not expected to be heavy today. He didn't have much of assignments and he could afford to sit in office and brood over the happenings of last 24 hours today. He was missing Nisha terribly and was damn worried about her. It was already around 9 a.m. He tried to indulge in reading newspaper but then finally decided that it is better to go out in the field and meet some of his 'sources' with whom he hadn't met for quite sometime.

Nisha walked out of the ICU ashen faced. Her aunt asked, "Is everything alright? Is he OK?"

"Yes, he is," she said.

"Aunty, can you sit here for a couple of hours. I have to go outside the hospital for some important work."

"Sure, don't worry. Give me your mobile phone number. If there is anything….I will call you," her aunt said.

Nisha went to the parking lot, took out her car and drove back to her home. She needed to think over all this and take a decision.

She reached home, parked the car, went to the kitchen, made a cup of green tea and went to the living room. She sipped the hot steaming herbal tea. It calmed her down. She sat on the sofa and rested her head on the back of sofa and closed her eyes.

Thoughts came and went away. Her mindspace resembled a typhoon initially but as the minutes ticked away, the storm died down, the tension evaporated and after two hours she opened her eyes.

Had she looked at her face in the mirror, she would have noticed a subtle change. There was steely resolve under the calmness of her soft and serene facial expressions. Brave hearts often react to tough challenges like that. And she was second to none. She had made up her mind.

She got up, washed her face, combed her hair and went back to the living room. She bolted the door carefully from inside and then flipped open her mobile. She had to talk to two most important people in her life—Pankaj and Lata.

The first call lasted for 12 minutes. She had talked to Pankaj. Before Pankaj could ask her anything, she told him, "Pankaj, I don't have much time. I trust you. I am sure you would not let me down. If you intend to, do let me know now."

"You can trust me Nisha, I am standing by you," Pankaj told her.

But he had no inkling what she was going to tell him.

"Now listen Pankaj, if you are really with me and if you really love me then you will do what I am going to tell you and she started speaking............."

Pankaj was dumbfounded. He was shocked to hear what she was telling him. The conversation finished in 12 minutes.

Nisha had a sigh of relief when the conversation ended with Pankaj telling her, "Whatever you say Nisha, whatever…."

Next call was to Lata which lasted for 8 minutes. Lata tried to argue in between, "You are mad, Nisha. Things don't work out this way…" Nisha interrupted her firmly and told her, "Lata, I have made the decision and for God's sake I am not asking you what is right and what is wrong, I am just asking you whether you are with me or not."

"I am with you Nisha," the conversation ended with Lata also putting a seal of approval on Nisha's plan of action, a bit reluctantly.

She had told both Pankaj and Lata that she would never be coming back to Delhi. She had decided to get married to Sandeep.

"I can't say no to my father, he is critical and if I don't honour his wish, he may not survive. I cannot live happily with anyone over the wishes of my dead father," she had told both Pankaj and Lata.

A pall of gloom had descended and overpowered Pankaj. Never ever in his life had he felt so low and he didn't know how to react. He felt on the verge of crying.

He didn't know what to do.

He was on the breakfast table when he had got Nisha's call. He had moved back to his room to take the call. After the call was finished, he sat for another half an hour trying to make sense of what had happened. He couldn't make sense out of it.

What pained him more than Nisha leaving him to get married to some guy of his father's choice was the realisation that Nisha would never be happy with him.

He picked up the phone and call Varun. "Are you free?"

"Always free for you. What are friends for?," Varun chuckled. Pankaj could hear blaring music behind him on the phone itself.

"Where are you?,"

"I am in gym *yaar*, tell me what happened? You are sounding very low."

"I am low. Can you meet me at the Rajouri Garden Metro Station in half an hour?"

"Sure, I will," Varun said with raised eyebrows. He was worried. He had never heard Pankaj speaking in such a jarred voice.

Both of them travelled to Pankaj's office in Varun's car where he explained to him what had happened in the morning.

Varun, for a change was serious, damn serious. His heart ached over the tragic turn of events which his friend was sharing with him. He knew that for a person like Pankaj, how devastating all this could be.

They had reached his office by the time, Pankaj's monologue finished. Pankaj was feeling a bit light initially when he shared all that he had to with his friend.

But then he suddenly started having the realisation that he has lost Nisha forever.

They were sitting in his car in front of his office and Varun was shocked to see tears rolling down Pankaj's eyes.

"Damn it! Why did this had to happen to a nice guy like you," he punched the dashboard of the car in anger buoyed by frustration.

As the window glasses as well as the front and back glass of the car were heavily tinted, almost black, so no one could see Pankaj crying except Varun.

They sat silent for a few minutes. Pankaj recollected himself, "Sorry yaar, shouldn't have cried, but can't help it," he said in a choked voice.

"Call up your boss and tell him you are not coming to office today," Varun told him.

"We will spend the day together, let us go for a long drive, we will go to Murthal (a place on the outskirts of Delhi) have some beer and lunch and talk about this, may be there could be a solution."

When Varun dropped Pankaj back at 11 p.m. in the night near his house, he realised that for the first time in life he couldn't offer a solution to a problem. Pankaj will have to suffer this and suffer it alone. Varun knew it, so did Pankaj, who felt a little drunk as he moved towards his house. He quietly sneaked into the house opening the door lock with an alternative key which he had and went to his room. He wanted to sleep, he was fatigued but his mind was racing like a F1 Formula Car reminding him again and again of all the moments he had spent together with Nisha. Liquor and loneliness is a deadly cocktail. Ask those who have tried it!

He crashed on the bed and switched on the TV. He didn't know when his physical fatigue overpowered his mind.

❑

22

Married. Happily??

What a bizarre day it was. It had rained and then there was bright sunshine. After sometime it started drizzling while there was full bright sunlight.

The weather God had perhaps decided that they would express their feelings. Things had moved pretty quickly during the last one week.

Purushottam Lal's situation had improved and he had been shifted to a private room in the hospital. He was recuperating but the doctors had told him, "Your heart is in pretty bad shape and it is better that you finish off all the pending tasks, keep yourself happy. You never know when the final call would come."

So to keep himself happy, Purushottam now insisted that Nisha should get married to Sandeep within a week.

Nisha had met Sandeep in hospital itself when he and his family came to meet Purushottam after they came to know that he was in hospital.

As soon as Purushottam got shifted to the room from the ICU, he had half an hour conversation behind closed doors with Sandeep's parents.

Nisha was standing outside trying to explain to Sandeep that she is ready to get married to him, only because her father wants her to do so.

"Frankly Sandeep, I have no feelings for you, in fact not for anyone now. I am just doing it because my father wants it. I don't want to lie to you so I have told you the truth."

Twenty-eight years old Sandeep Kumar, a Junior Engineer in PWD, was smiling all through just saying two words, "I understand".

"I hope you understand that I can't be like others even if we get married," Nisha told him.

"*Hm*......," came the reply from Sandeep. He had a wheatish complexion, curly hair and strong arms. It appeared that he was fond of going to gym and used strong deodorants.

The door of the room opened and the old couple came out of the room. They seemed happy, so happy as if they were ready to fly without wings. The woman, Sandeep's mother, whose name was Kamla, hugged Nisha, "Oh! I am so happy that such a beautiful girl is going to be my daughter-in-law."

Surprisingly, Nisha didn't feel anything. She just kept staring at her. Sandeep, smiled sheepishly. His father, Rajendra Kumar stood there trying to hide his gleeful smile realising that Nisha's father was still unwell and one shouldn't be too loud in terms of expressing their happiness.

"Your father wants to talk to you, we will wait here," he said.

Nisha got herself free from that suffocating hug and quietly went inside the room. Her father was still lying there on the bed.

He spoke to her with great effort in a very low voice which was barely audible. "They are a good family. As you know doctors have told me that anything can happen to me anytime now and my heart is not in a very good shape, so I want you to get married to Sandeep within next two days. It will be a simple marriage ceremony, day after tomorrow in the Arya Samaj Temple and then when I will be out of hospital, I will hold a grand reception ceremony where we will call all the guests."

He was expecting some resistance but was pleasantly surprised to find none.

"One more thing, you will have to speak to Shekhar. I guess he will reach here by tonight. You know he doesn't talk to me much. He will have to do the "*Kanyadaan*" ceremony as I can't be out of hospital in a week's time. From our family, Shekhar and your aunt (mother's sister) and her family will attend the marriage ceremony. Sandeep's family is likely to invite a couple of close family friends to attend this ceremony."

"Hmmm….OK, Papa, now you take rest. You need rest. I will take care of everything," she replied.

Purushottam was already feeling tired as he had to make a huge effort to speak. The drowsiness caused by the medicines he was taking did rest of the work. He fell asleep.

Nisha looked at him for a minute. She came out. An extraordinary engagement ceremony followed in next three minutes. Kamla had taken a gold ring out of her finger and Rajendra too had taken out his diamond ring from one of his fingers. Sandeep pushed the diamond ring on Nisha's finger and Nisha repeated the act for Sandeep as if a robot was doing it. Her hands did not shake at all, not even a nerve inside her flinched. She was perfectly calm like dead sea.

"We will meet at 11 a.m. day after tomorrow at Arya Samaj Temple near your house. If you need anything let us know. We will send the wedding *saree* for you by tomorrow and the jewellery too which you have to wear. Please call us if you need anything. You are a part of our family now," Rajendra said. And the trio left the place.

Nisha sat on a bench outside the private room for a while and then went inside. She suddenly felt exhausted and closed her eyes with a deep breath while sitting on a sofa-cum-bed inside the room which was meant to be used by attendants who stay with the patient during day and night.

She didn't know when she dozed off. Suddenly she felt a familiar touch on her forehead and opened her eyes like a camera shutterbug. A few inches away from her was a blurred face and in split second she realised it was Shekhar.

"She got up and as if the silence between the two spoke, they came out of the private room to talk about the incidents of the past few days."

Nisha didn't cry, nor did she appear emotional at all. She spoke and explained to her brother about the events of the past few days.

He was shocked. He was shocked, less because of his father's sudden illness but more because of the fact that how her sister was turning herself into a sacrificial goat.

"How can you do that Nisha, you don't even know this guy. We don't know who they are. You know how we hate our father's choices."

The bitterness within him was oozing out with every word that came out from his lips. "He only thinks about himself. Only you and I know this. And what about Pankaj. I thought you liked him and both of you will ultimately get married. I haven't met him but whatever you told me about him makes me feel, he is a good guy."

"I have already taken the decision *bhaiyya* and I have told Pankaj also. I will never be happy with him if I get married to him against our father's wishes."

"Pankaj is a very good human being and he deserves better than living with a person like me who would probably carry the weight of unfulfilled wishes of a dying father. I would be happy with him but I would never be able to give him the happiness which he really deserves. He will surely find someone who doesn't carry the kind of emotional baggage I would carry if I walk over the wishes of my sick father."

Nisha said it all as if it was the last time she was speaking her mind to someone, "Just Imagine *bhaiyya*, If I say "No" to our father and he dies here. Can I ever live normally with that kind of guilt consciousness? If you were in my place, will you not blame yourself for the death of our father deep inside your heart where logic doesn't apply. Deep inside we all know what truth is. "

Shekhar stood speechless for a few seconds and then said quietly, "Nisha, you are my sister and I will do anything that makes you happy. You do what you feel is the right thing for you. It doesn't matter what others thinks about this and I will stand by you."

Nisha, just held his hand and pressed it warmly with a painful smile, "Hey don't worry, I will be fine."

Thirty six hours after this, Nisha was a married woman.

❑

23

Two Weeks Later

All hell broke loose. Nisha was stunned. She had a huge cut on her upper lip and it was bleeding profusely. Her white Tee shirt was torn. And the right side of her face was swollen. She had bruises all over her forearms.

The man who did this was standing outside the bathroom door yelling, shouting and insanely pleading—all in bits and pieces with no specific sequence. In between, there was a barrage of abuses directed at her from the same man. It was an attached bathroom to their bedroom. She realised now what kind of a chauvinist pig her husband was.

Though she had told him that she didn't have any feelings for him but still after getting married she had told Lata, "I will give it a chance. Sandeep can't be Pankaj but still I will give it a chance. All I need is some time."

She had spent last couple of weeks mostly in the hospital and it was only two days ago that his father was discharged from the hospital and sent back home. He was much better now and seemed to be ready to resume his normal routine. Shekhar had taken the train back to reach his institute, the day their father went back home from the hospital. He was not ready to spend even a single night at her father's house. His hatred for his father had reached to a point of no-return after he had to do "*Kanyadaan*" for his sister. He knew how she was sacrificing her life for the whims and fancies of his father and he too had contributed to that now, though, very unwillingly.

The day Nisha came back from her father's house, she was tired and slept early. In the middle of the night she suddenly woke up as she felt something was crawling over her breasts. It was Sandeep's hand. She sat up with a jerk and switched on the bedside lamp. "What are you doing Sandeep?," she was extremely annoyed."

"You remember, I had told you something on the first night after our marriage when you tried to do the same thing. I am telling you the same thing again that I need some time to be close to you. Give me some time."

Sandeep spoke in a ice-cold voice, "Look Nisha, you are my wife and every married couple has sex. I know you are scared as you haven't done it before, even I am a virgin. So let's do it." He tried to force himself on her again.

A man full of lust is worst than an injured demon fighting for his life. As he tried to hold her forcibly by waist, she somehow managed to wriggle out of his grip and rest of the night was spent in bitter arguments. Infact it was more of a monologue full of venom with Sandeep fuming and cursing and swearing that if she doesn't know that going to bed with him was her duty as a wife than he would make her realise that.

That day it all ended with arguments. But today, it was different. The sequence of events had the same beginning. But the ending was much more terrible. When she tried to resist his advances, the initial reaction was a vulgar abuse hurled at her by Sandeep.

She protested. He reacted.

Slap!

She was stunned.

Another slap! This resulted in a deep cut over her upper lip.

He was blinded by lust and refused to see this.

"Don't do it," she screamed as he tried to rip her Tee shirt.

She was able to push him back for a moment and he lost his balance and fell hitting the bed post.

He got up in a swift movement as a terrified Nisha was looking for a safe corner in that room.

Then her real ordeal began."

She was screaming and he was trying to torn her clothes and hitting her wherever he could.

By God's grace, a knock on the door came. Rajendra and Kamla had heard the shouts and screams.

"What's happening?," Kamla asked.

"Nothing Mama, it is just a husband and wife argument. Nisha is very angry. I am trying to calm her down," Sandeep told them in a loud voice from inside the room.

"Don't fight like this. Even the neighbours can probably hear this. Why don't you try and sort it out calmly?," Rajendra sermonised to his son and daughter-in-law, standing outside the closed door.

"OK Papa, we will do that. Don't worry. We are fine. You go and sleep, it is already midnight," Sandeep convinced them and the old couple walked away thinking it is just another typical fight between husband and wife and confined only to the arguments.

"I tell you, the youngsters these days just do not have any patience," Rajendra said ruefully while turning his back and moving towards his bedroom. Kamla was following her.

Nisha had taken full advantage of Sandeep's attention being diverted by this conversation. She rushed to the bathroom and bolted the door from inside while Sandeep was busy talking to his parents.

As she looked at her battered face in the bathroom mirror tears started rolling down her face.

She used the cotton and antiseptic solution in bathroom cabinet and was able to stop the bleeding. She took off her Tee and put on another Tee which she had put for washing in a pile of dirty clothes in a bucket there earlier during the day. It was not so clean but aleast it was better than the one which had been turned into a rag by her husband.

She kept herself locked inside the bathroom till wee hours of morning. It was around 3 a.m. in the morning when she came out of the bathroom after hearing the loud snoring of Sandeep. He was sleeping as if there was no worry on his head. She was in a hurry as if there is no tomorrow.

She had spent almost three hours in the bathroom. The first half an hour was spent by her to stop the bleeding and change clothes. The second half an hour was spent by her to calm down her nerves. And the next two hours were spent by her thinking about what all she has done with her life and what needed to be done.

Reality had finally dawned on her and she came out of bathroom with a resolve. She had realised during these three hours that she had committed a blunder by succumbing to the whims of her father.

While standing in front of the bathroom mirror her innerself told her, “You have committed a mistake Nisha. I warned you. Nevertheless your intentions were not wrong. Your heart was at the right place. But now you must have realised that you have only one life and you have already spent almost a quarter of that. Your first duty is towards yourself. You must make yourself happy and do what makes you happy. Do whatever it takes to make you happy. If you don’t do that you are not respecting your life, you are not respecting your existence and you are not respecting your being. That is sacrilege. So go ahead and make yourself happy. Those who love you will understand and those who don’t, it’s their problem not yours”.

After a long long time, Nisha smiled. Her lips hurt when she smiled. The decision had been made. She felt fortunate that she still had someone she could turn to.

At 3:30 a.m., Nisha quietly left the house. She had a small leather wallet with Rs 2000, all her credit cards and her mobile phone. As if God was out there waiting for her, a lone auto-rickshaw was visible to her. She got into it without giving a second thought and told the auto-rickshaw driver, a turbaned, man in sixties, "Will you take me to Inter State Bus Terminal. I have to catch a bus to Delhi."

The stars were twinkling and the moon was moving gradually to hide itself behind the cloud cover which was had shades of grey. The dawn was about to break. Nobody has ever been able to stop it, no body will. She got into a Haryana Roadways Bus which left Chandigarh's Inter State Bus Terminal at 4 a.m. sharp.

She waited for her wrist watch to show 5 a.m. and then started sending text messages from her cell phone.

The first message was to her father.

"Papa, I am leaving Sandeep's house. I am going back to Delhi. I can't live with him. You can ask him why? From my side I can tell you that I want to be happy and I can't be happy with him and I can't sacrifice my life for you."

The second message was to Sandeep. "I am leaving. Don't try to contact me or trouble my family or I will lodge a police case against you."

The third message was to her brother. "Shekhar, you were right. I can't be happy with anyone else except…you know☺. So I am leaving everything and taking a chance to make myself happy. I am safe. Don't worry, I will contact you soon."

Then she made two calls. The first one was to Lata. She simply told her, "Don't ask anything, I am coming to Delhi. Come over to pick me up at 9 a.m. at ISBT at Kashmere Gate at the spot where all the buses from Chandigarh arrive."

She took a deep breath and made a last call. Pankaj picked up the phone. He was half-asleep, still not able to take Nisha off his mind. "Hey, are you all right, you are calling so early in the morning?," his voice acted as a soothing balm. Tears rolled down her eyes with a wide smile. The lips didn't hurt that much now.

Nisha's voice was a little quivered as she explained to him all that had happened. Pankaj listened with a rage building inside him. He wanted to break Sandeep's neck. But before he could react, Nisha said, "Pankaj, will you marry me, will you spend your life with me? Say Yes or No and don't think. Say what you feel like. I know this is not the way one should ask such questions but I still feel I can take that much liberty with you. And I am sorry, but I need your answer right now".

❑

24

Final Call

Pankaj had never seen his parents so traumatised. A few hours later at the breakfast table, he broke the news to his parents that there is someone he is in love with and would like to get married to her.

They were happy. But when their son explained that Nisha was married and that she had walked out of her marriage, they were scandalised.

He tried to explain to them that for him it doesn't matter even if she was married for few days. But his parents refused to accept her outrightly and told him that they would not accept his decision.

He told them bluntly, "I am still going to get married to her."

His mother tried to intervene but Manohar stopped her and put it across to his beloved son plainly, "Look Pankaj, we love you, but we have certain respect in society. I am open-minded and so is your mother. We would have readily accepted anyone but not a married girl who has walked out of her marriage within days. You do what you want to do but this girl is not coming to my house. And that is my final decision."

His mother followed his father as both of them got up and moved to their bedroom.

Pankaj quietly went to his room, picked up all his certificates and necessary documents and then placed a call to a retired IAS officer Neelesh Prasad from his mobile phone.

"Hi Pankaj, how are you?"

"I am fine Sir, I need your help."

"Tell me Pankaj, I will do whatever I can, you know how fond I was of you."

Neelesh Prasad's only son had committed suicide 20 years ago when he had not allowed him to marry a girl who belonged to a different caste. His wife died soon after, not able to take the blow and he spent the rest of his life in the corridors of power. These twin tragedies had transformed this honest officer into a man full of bitterness towards everything around him. Everyone around him knew that he was a difficult man to get along with. No journalist tried to meet him as he was completely inaccessible to anyone outside the four walls of his office.

Somehow he had developed a liking for Pankaj when he met him the first time at am official dinner organised by Neelesh's boss in the Ministry of Home Affairs. Pankaj's passion and sincerity reminded him of his son. Pankaj too had become fond of this old man who was considered to be notorious for his vicious attitude towards media persons. They gradually developed a special bond. They discussed films, music, books and politics for hours. He invited Pankaj often to his house also. They never talked about news stories. Pankaj never asked for any information from him. He just liked this old man.

Neelesh had retired last year and was now settled in the hill station of Mussoorie. To keep himself occupied he had accepted the offer to be the of principle of a prestigious boarding school there which was run by a trust comprising of mainly retired bureaucrats.

Pankaj had visited him once at his school and over a cup of coffee. Neelesh had told him, "If you ever want to teach and settle here, let me know. There is a dearth of good teachers and kids need young people like you."

"Of course you would not leave the glamorous job of a journalist. Still if you ever feel like becoming a teacher, come here. This is the right place for people like you. Teaching kids is the most important thing and we as a country have been neglecting this aspect of nation building. The best talent doesn't go for teaching."

Pankaj remembered that conversation. He ran that whole conversation in his mind again in fast forward mode. Neelesh picked up his call on third ring. Pankaj explained to him over the next 20 minutes the whole situation.

He could hear stunned silence from the other side.

Then a voice came, "Pankaj, I have lost one son. I don't want that to happen to any father or mother. They may not agree with you right now but they will agree with you. Even if they don't, you have a right to live with the love of your life. Come over son, I can't match your salary but I have two posts lying vacant. We are looking for an English teacher for senior classes and another one to teach Business Studies. I think you can teach English and Nisha can teach Business Studies. We will give you accommodation and a salary of Rs 22,000 each. Both of you can join from day after tomorrow".

"Thanks a lot Sir, I will be there, I am leaving the city with Nisha tonight."

"By the way, the education for your children would be total free of cost. That is the school policy," Neelesh chuckled.

❑❑❑